The Five Di

Make the sexual experience in your marriage what it is meant to be

By

Kenneth Edward Barnes

Contents

Introduction

Part 1: The First Dimension of Sex
Chapter 1: The Analytical Aspect of Sex
Chapter 2: Human Sexual Reproduction
Chapter 3: How does it Work?

Part 2: The Second Dimension of Sex
Chapter 1: The Sexual Awakening
Chapter 2: Why are these Changes Necessary?

Part 3: The Third Dimension of Sex
Chapter 1: Animalistic Lust
Chapter 2: The Shape of Things to Come
Chapter 3: Getting Down to Basics
Chapter 4: Getting in the Mood
Chapter 5: I Can't Get No Satisfaction!

Part 4: The Fourth Dimension of Sex
Chapter 1: Finding Love
Chapter 2: What's Love Got to Do with It?
Chapter 3: Poem: What is Love?
Chapter 4: Love for a Husband
Elizabeth's Poem
Elizabeth's Letter
Chapter 5: Love for a Wife
Poem: A Treasure:
Chapter 6: Poem: My Dearest
Chapter 7: Poem: Will You?
Chapter 8: Poem: An Angel that came to Me
Chapter 9: Poem: The Price of You
Chapter 10: What is a Wife?

Part 5: The Fifth Dimension of Sex
Chapter 1: What is the Fifth Dimension of Sex?
Chapter 2: The Beginning of Sex
Chapter 3: God Commands Us to Have Sex
Chapter 4: Why Marriage?
Chapter 5: How Can You Have This Special Love?
Chapter 6: Tackling the Problems
Chapter 7: The Unfaithful Mate
Chapter 8: The Joy of Sex
About the Author
Other Books by the Author

Introduction

Everyone reading these words came into the world because of sex. As difficult as it may be to believe, your parents had sexual intercourse and conceived you. This is a biological fact. A few may have been artificially conceived, but that is the exception. I will be discussing the "natural way" humans have sex and why.

Nearly all creatures on earth reproduce by having sex. Birds, animals, reptiles, amphibians, fish, and insects all reproduce by sex. Animals, however, do not think about why they have sex or what it is for, they are programmed by instinct to know how to court, mate and raise their young. Humans, on the other hand, try to figure out how to court, how to have sex and sometimes ponder the reasons why.

We are the only species that does not know how to have sex unless we are taught and often we are given the wrong information. If left alone on our own, we might be able to figure out how to reproduce with the opposite sex, but without knowledge that has been passed down we would most likely just "mate" very much like animals do. We are unique among all creatures on earth and we are the only ones that can consciously contemplate the why of things and go beyond what has been programmed into all other life forms.

Sex is a topic we all love to read about. We want sex in our marriage to be good or even better than it is. There are different levels of sex and that is why I wrote this book. Most only know of a couple, the animalistic view and the loving relationship view. This little book of about 27,500 words tells you how it can be greater.

I have written this short book of about 28,500 words to try to help married couples have a closer and more fulfilling relationship. If you do not have a good relationship outside the bedroom, most likely you will not have a good sexual relationship either. On the other hand, if your sex life is a disappointment it can cause the entire relationship to suffer and maybe even fail.

Even if you are not married but hope to be, the information in this book can be important. You should know before you are married how to make your sexual relationship good.

In the book, I discuss ways to have better sex and why this is important. I will be discussing adult topics, but in a loving, monogamous, marital relationship. I will also say why this is important. There are problems that all couples have in marriage and these can and do affect their sexual relationship. I will address these problems also and show ways to deal with them.

Today, many have so much misinformation, either given to them by their parents, friends or by others. Often the ones giving the advice are confused themselves about the topic. There are others, which are even appalled about sex because of bad experiences or wrong information they have received.

I will try to show that human sex is on a much higher plain than any other creature on earth and why. I will discuss human sexual desires, and what role men and women have in fulfilling each other's sexual needs, thus providing a fulfilled sexual relationship.

I will take you from the analytical aspect of sex, the awaking of sexual desires, animalistic lust and then on to the sex we call love. Finally, I will take you to another dimension, the fifth dimension of sex.

Why am I qualified to write this book? I have been married for most of my life, a total of over 42 years. Because of a divorce, that I did not want, and the death of another very loving spouse I have went through a lot of grief. Besides being married for many years, while I was single I talked for many long hours with hundreds of women about relationships and why they work or don't. I have also studied the Bible since I was 14-years-old and now I'm over 64-years of age. I know what God has said how relationships and marriage are supposed to work. I am also a church ordained Messianic Rabi. That means a "teacher" that believes that Christ was and is not only the Savior of Christians but also the Messiah of the Jews and all other humans on earth. God is the one that created male and female; He is also the one that instituted marriage and has told us how and why we are to have sex. In His word, He tells us how we are to act towards one another in a loving relationship. This information, along with what I have learned from not only reading and listening to others about the subject, but what I have lived, makes me qualified to write what I have found.

Part 1:
The First Dimension of Sex

Sex is universal among nearly every living thing. Only germs, bacteria and other single cell life forms multiply without sex. Mammals, birds, reptiles, amphibians, fish, most sea life and even insects and arachnids (spiders) have sex.

We are very fortunate that we are not like some creatures that reproduce. The praying mantis female usually devours the male after he has mated with her and often before he is finished. While she is eating his head, he may still be inside her fertilizing the eggs for the next generation. His mission has been fulfilled, and now he is of no use, except as protein for the female and her eggs. The same goes for the black widow spider. The tiny male must carefully and cautiously sneak up behind her, calm her, then mate. As soon as he is done, he must make a mad dash to safety before she turns on him and has him for her lunch.

Courtship and mating among birds and animals can be fascinating and this is true even with humans. Therefore, in this first part of the book, we will look at sex just as a biological function of animals and humans. This view of sex, the analytical view, is the first dimension. There is no engaging in sex, we only see it from a distance.

Chapter 1

The Analytical Aspect of Sex

The first dimension of sex is the discussion we are having about it. It is the study or discussion about sex, courtship and reproduction in nearly all life forms, including humans. This will be an analytical look in a biological sense. We will touch on how the human reproductive system works, which is the foundation of sex. I will also mention how some animals court and mate. We can learn a lot from nature, and many birds and animals have fascinating behaviors when it comes to sex.

The lowest forms of life that have sex are the insects. All mate then the female lays eggs. When the young hatch, they are usually on their own. Some of the social insects such as ants, termites and wasps care for their young and they all live together in a social society. The arachnids lay eggs, but they often care for their young by guarding them. Some spiders even carry their young on their back for a while after they hatch.

Most fish lay eggs and the male fertilizes them by squirting his sperm or milt in the water above them. A few fish, like sharks, mate and the female carries the young inside and gives live birth.

Amphibians mate and lay eggs, usually in water. One species of frog lays eggs, but the male carries the eggs on his back in special "pockets" until the tadpoles hatch and develop to a stage where they can breathe on their own.

Reptiles mate and most lay eggs. A few snakes do give live birth, however. Most of the reptiles abandon the eggs after they are laid, like the turtles, which bury them in sand or soil. Some of the crocodilian family lay their eggs in mounds of decaying compost and guard their young. They even help the young out of the nest when they hatch and then carry them to the water where they continue guarding them until they are more able to care for themselves.

All birds mate and lay eggs, but some types are a little different. The gallinaceous birds, (chicken like birds) lay a large clutch of eggs in a nest, usually on the ground. Soon after hatching, the young are able to follow their mother, who guards them, keeps them warm and helps show them how to find food. Ducks, geese and many shore birds raise their young in a similar way. The brush turkey or mound bird builds a large mound of decomposing vegetation, where she lays her eggs. The male tends it, taking compost off or adding it to keep the temperature correct until the eggs hatch. Once hatched, the young birds are totally independent of their parents and take care of themselves.

Passerines, (perching birds) like robins, crows and many others, lay their eggs in a nest in a tree or sometimes on the ground. Their young are more helpless when born and the parents must feed them until they are feathered out, can fly and are capable of finding food on their own.

The pigeon family, which includes doves, lays only one or two eggs in a very flimsy nest. The nest is in a tree or bush. The rock dove (common pigeon) makes its nest on clefts in the wild or feral pigeons build on man-made structures, such as bridges, buildings or barns. The pigeon family is unique in a couple of ways. They drink water by sucking it up, while other birds tip up their heads to let the water run down their throats. They also are unique in the way they feed their young. Both parents fed the offspring with "pigeon milk", a substance that is produced in the pigeon's crop. The parents regurgitate this into the young bird's mouth.

Mammals all mate and most carry their young in a womb until birth. The marsupials like kangaroos, Tasmanian devils and opossums, give live birth, but the young are premature and must crawl into a pouch where they attach themselves to a nipple until they develop further. The opossum (Didelphis Virginiana) is the only marsupial in North America. The scientific name means "double womb one from Virginia." Besides the females having a double womb and a pouch, the males are rather strange too. The male opossum has a penis that has two heads, which is for the double womb of the female. His testicles are above the penis instead of under it like all other mammals. The testicles are also a pretty blue in color.

The monotremes, which consist of only two species, the duckbill platypus and the echidna or spiny anteater, are the only mammals that lay eggs.

Most mammals, from the tiny pygmy shrew to the great blue whale, mate, carry their young in a single womb, give birth and nurse their young from mammillary glands that are on the outside of their body.

Each kind of mammal has a little different way of finding a mate, courting, copulating and raising their offspring. We will look at a few of the ways animals court and mate a little later in the third dimension of sex.

Chapter 2

Human Sexual Reproduction

The human reproductive process is also very fascinating, even when we look at just the biological facts.

Maybe you can remember when you were in school and sat in Biology class. Textbooks showed the human reproduction system and how it works. The adult female has *ovaries,* which produce an egg each month. Usually one ovary produces an egg one month then the next month the other ovary produces one. Sometimes both will produce an egg. If a woman happens to conceive a child during one of these times when both ovaries produce an egg, she can have twins. The twins, however, will not be identical and will look like any other child that she may have if she had conceived them separately. If a woman conceives twins with only one egg, it will have been fertilized by two sperm. In this case, she can have two boys, two girls, or one boy and one girl and they will be identical twins. The sex of the baby is determined by the male's sperm and the chromosomes in it.

From the ovaries, there is a *fallopian tube* that goes to the uterus in which the egg travels. If she happens to conceive, the egg attaches to the side of the *uterus* and the baby begins to develop. If she does not conceive, she will have a menstrual period. During this time, the tissue and the blood vessels that have built up during the past month lining the uterus will slough off and the egg will be discarded. This menstrual period will usually last from between three and seven days. The cycle will then repeat itself until the woman goes through menopause or "the change".

This is the biological way a woman becomes pregnant. The man is very different. As a male becomes able to produce sperm, which varies but is usually when he's around the age of twelve or thirteen, he is physically old enough to father a child.

The male reproductive system is very complex. Each day the man will produce millions of sperm in the *testicles*, which are stored there. A tube called the *vas deferens* carries sperm from each testicle to the *urethra*. In the prostate gland and *seminal vesicles,* a white looking fluid is produced and stored and is mixed with the sperm in the vas deferens. During ejaculation, the sperm, along with the whitish fluid, is expelled trough the urethra and out of the body.

When a man becomes aroused, there are tiny valves at the base of the penis that open and let blood flow into it allowing the penis to swell and become rigid. This is so it will be able to enter the female and accomplish what nature intended.

Most of the time, the penis is not inflated, and is in a flaccid state. It only becomes erect when the man is aroused. We will discuss this later.

. An interesting note is that the skin on a man's scrotum is unique and different from any other human skin. When it gets cold, the skin draws up, which pulls the testicles closer to the body to keep them warm? When the temperature gets warm, the skin relaxes and lets the testicles drop down away from the body so they will be cool. This is because the testicles need to be a few degrees cooler than the body to better produce sperm. The skin on the vagina of the woman is the same type of skin that is on the lips. If there is ever a need for a skin graft to the lips, the vaginal tissue can be used.

Now back to sexual intercourse. During sexual intercourse, the male's sperm will be released during ejaculation. If there is an egg present, only one sperm will likely fertilize it. Occasionally two sperm will reach the egg (as I mentioned above), get inside at the same time, and twins will be born.

Now, before a couple gets to that point a lot of things have happened. We will discuss how and why in the following chapters. There was courtship, foreplay (hopefully) and then the actions that got the couple to reach the place I just described.

What I have described above is about all your high school biology books and teacher told you and maybe not that much.

This is one look at sex in an analytical view. The next chapter will look a little further into the biological aspect of sex when it takes the next step towards the second dimension.

Chapter 3

How does it Work?

In order for sex to work correctly, there are several steps that need to be taken. I will go into more detail in a later chapter when sex is viewed in an animalistic way.

When a boy starts to go through puberty, many changes take place. There are outward changes and there are changes that take place inside the body. These changes are more apparent outside than in, but the changes in his mind are just as real.

I have not read anywhere about what happens before a boy goes through puberty. It is not morally correct or ethical to study sex in children, but I was a child and I can remember a few things that happened to me while growing up.

The first event was when I was about eight-years-old. I liked climbing trees and often would shinny up a tall, slender sapling in our front yard. The first time this event happened it surprised me. Starting up the tree, I clamped my knees against the side of the tree and pushed my way up. Each time I squeezed my legs tight against the tree I pushed myself higher. After several times of this squeezing and pushing I suddenly had an overwhelming urge. This intense feeling was so great that I had to slide down the tree and hold my privates until the feeling subsided. I didn't know what it was at the time, but I instinctively knew it had something to do with sex. I remember saying to myself "I wish I had a girl here." At that age, I would not have known what to do, but something inside told me that this feeling had something to do with the opposite sex.

When a boy has an organism before he reaches puberty it is more like what a woman experiences. There is no ejaculation, only an orgasm. The organisms also can come one after the other (at least up to ten) until they run together into one long one. The intensity, however, fades and the peaks of organism are very low. The feeling, however, is intense, something like the tree incident.

When a boy first begins to go through puberty, his sexual organs will start producing the lubricant that he will need during sexual relations as an adult. A year or so later, there will be a few sperm show up with this lubricant during orgasm and ejaculation. This is when he'll know he could father a child.

The female, also, will start producing the same type of lubricant when she enters puberty and starts her menstrual cycles.

When the young boy or girl begins to change into a man or woman not only does their bodies go through great changes, their minds will also be affected. Now on to the next dimension.

Part 2:
The Second Dimension of Sex

The first dimension was the analytical look at sex. During this next part, I will discuss the second dimension of sex, the Sexual Awaking. This section will focus on the changes in the human body, both male and female. Also in this dimension, I will discuss the awaking of our sexual desires.

When does this happen? Why does this happen? What does it mean?

Chapter 1

The Sexual Awakening

This desire first manifests itself with the urge to be near the opposite sex. Sometimes this can be very early in life, but at a very early age, it is not actually associated with any sexual desire. It will be just the beginning of an interest in the opposite sex.

When the sexual awaking actually begins, the human body and mind, both male and female, will start to drastically change. In males, it may start out with uncontrollable erections at any time of the day or night. In addition, it can happen without warning or it can be triggered by a thought or by some visual stimulation. This visual stimulation can be a look at an attractive female or even a picture of her. At this time in the boy's life, there can also be a racing pulse, blushing and/or sweaty palms when he gets near a girl that he is attracted to. This change in the male begins at different ages but usually begins between the ages of eleven to thirteen. Besides his thought patterns changing, he will begin to grow hair on his face, as well as elsewhere. His voice, too, will begin to get lower. When his voice starts changing there may be days where he is talking in a deep voice and suddenly it will crack and revert to the high-pitched voice he had before, which can be rather embarrassing. Going through puberty can be a very awkward time for boys. This is especially true when he begins to have the uncontrollable erections that can happen anywhere and at any time.

As soon as these changes begin, boys will notice that the girls look prettier and most of the time he will want to be near them (unless he is extremely bashful or shy). Even if the boys are too shy to associate with girls, they will still want to. They will also notice several things about the opposite sex that they had not paid much attention to before.

As for the girls, they will begin to get curves and start developing breasts and when they look at you and smile, you sometimes get butterflies in your stomach.

The girls begin to feel more feminine and like to dress up and usually have the desire to wear make up to make themselves look more attractive. They also pay much more attention to their bodies because they are rapidly changing. Usually this is when their mothers have a talk with them about what is happening to their bodies and what will happen in the future. In the past, many mothers were embarrassed to talk with their daughters about this. This is shameful because little girls can suddenly start their monthly cycles without warning, which can frighten them. I know of several girls that this happened to. There should be nothing embarrassing or shameful about a natural body function that happens to every woman on earth. It is the mother's responsibility to discuss this fact of life with their daughter "before" it takes place.

Once the girl begins turning into an adult and understands what is happening, she should feel good about herself. She is coming of age, she is changing into a mature woman, she has a lot to look forward to. Many times, however, there is a lot of pressure on them. They may feel ugly or awkward, or fat. They need to understand that nature knows what it is doing. They also need to know why nature is doing this to them. That is one reason I am writing this book. I am a man and have been so for nearly 64 years. I have seen hundreds of thousands of women in my life. I have seen about the same number of men and know their reactions around women. I know what men like to see when they look at a woman. They love to see curves. They do not want to see bones sticking out as if the women are sick. The biological fact of life is that men are programmed to "want" a woman that can bear them children. Nature has designed this "image of a woman" in their mind so that they will want to have sex with her. If she has large breasts to feed offspring, if she has wide, curvy hips to bear children he will be attracted. If she looks ill, weak, or frail he is more apt not to want to have sex with her. I will talk more about this in the third dimension, which is "Animalistic Lust."

Chapter 2

Why are these Changes Necessary?

All these changes in boys and girls are to prepare them for adulthood and for the perpetuation of their kind. It is so they can someday have sex and reproduce. This is what every species on earth does. I heard someone once say, "No one ever died by not having sex." That is untrue. You can only live for three or four minutes without air; you can live a few days without water; and you can live a few weeks without food before you die. You can live for years without sex, but unless you have sex and reproduce yourself, you will die and your kind will cease. All species of animal life on earth breaths air to live. Every specie drinks water to live. Each specie eats food to live, and every specie has sex so they will not become extinct.

Sex is the ultimate goal. To have sex and carry on the specie is the reason they breathe, eat, and drink. Most care for their young until the young can care for themselves. Then the parents have fulfilled their mission and that is to have produced themselves through their young.

Part 3:
The Third Dimension of Sex

The third dimension is like shifting into third gear in a racecar, for this is where we make first contact with the opposite sex. The physical connection with another of your kind in a sexual way is exhilarating but can also be a little frightening at first.

The first contact is usually the embrace and or kiss. Most of the time, this first "real" kiss is remembered for life. The next step is touching, and then the actual sex act. This third dimension often times is as far as some will ever go. It is the same dimension that animals have. It is the raw sexual desire for the opposite sex and the fulfilment of that desire. It is controlled by the mental and physical sexual desires and needs we have for a man or woman.

This animalistic urge and desire is not bad because it is given to make you want to mate with the opposite sex so you can reproduce. All animals have this and without it all life would cease to exist.

In this section, we will go into more detail of how the human body is made and how it works before, during and after sexual intercourse. This part of the book will be much more explicit and is intended to help married couples understand how the human body is designed for this basic instinct.

Chapter 1

Animalistic Lust!

When any wild or even domesticated animal reaches maturity, it has an instinct to mate and produce offspring to perpetuate its own kind. Each specie has rules it follows in order to be successful at reproducing. Some male birds put on displays to attract a mate. Male deer, bison and other hoofed animals fight each other for the right to breed with the females. After the male is successful, there is a courtship. Sometimes it is simple and other times it is much more elaborate.

When a male sheep (ram) wins the favor of a ewe, he uses his front leg (that he stiffens) to strike the female on her side to let her know he is ready to mate with her. If she's ready, she stands still, he mounts her, and it is over in a couple of seconds. That's all there is to it.

On the other hand, when cranes court, they bow to one another, throw their heads back, then leap into the air, flopping their wings in an elegant dance.

Certain species of grebes actually run on the surface of water, side-by-side, with their necks held in a graceful pose in a choreographed courtship display.

Doves and pigeons display to the females by cooing and tail dragging, as they make short runs to impress her. After he is accepted as her mate, they preen each other's face, which resembles kissing. Then they go through an act, which resembles the way they feed young. They lock bills and shutter as if they are regurgitating food into the mouth of their offspring.

Humans court, they sometimes dance, there are even cases of the males fighting over the females, but there are no set rules as there are with wild animals. Gorillas beat their chest to frighten off rival males. Frogs and toads puff up to make themselves look bigger and more frightening, but men must resort more often than not to other things.

We have been domesticated for so long that we do not rely on instincts much anymore. There are some instincts, however, that are still there under the surface and they sometimes come out. I will speak about these later.

When a male animal meets or even sees a female of its own kind, it has the instinct to try and mate with her. If she is in season, he will automatically know what to do, be it a grizzly bear, a crocodile or a snail. Men are no different. If they see a desirable female, they have inborn instincts that make him want to come near her. First, he must look to see if there are any rival males. Then he must approach cautiously as not to frighten her away. If she does not run, he can then proceed to court her. He may be driven away, however, if she does not approve of his looks, his smell, or any other undesirable traits. This is the way nature works for almost ever male of every species. It is the female that decides if the male is right for her. He is just wanting to find a desirable female to mate with. This is because he is driven to do so by the raging hormones that are being produced in his body. He doesn't have much control over his fate. Male salmon will swim thousands of miles, across oceans, up streams, go up waterfalls, pass a gauntlet of hungry bears and dozens of anglers just to release his sperm. After he spawns, he goes belly up, and dies. He dies because he has fulfilled his biological purpose. Thankfully, this doesn't happen to humans. Well, most of the time it doesn't.

I have said this with humor, but it's true. Nearly all men have this great desire to have sex with a female. As soon as they begin to turn into a man the hormones in their body causes them to have the urge to have sex. This is just a fact of life. The only problem is that we are not wild animals. We are, however, somewhat like other animals and do have rules to follow in courtship and mating, only they are set more by culture than by biological needs or desires.

Why do men and even adolescent males desire a female? Boys from an early age are preprogrammed to want sex. All the equipment is there and is waiting to be turned on. There is an incident that happened to me when I was only six or seven years old that explains this. We lived in a small house when I was that age. When everyone was in bed asleep (or so our parents thought), they would make love. I could not see what was going on in the dark, but I could hear. I very well remember my mother making certain sounds, which did something to my mind and even body. I didn't understand it, but I do remember what I felt and thought. I can still remember thinking, "I can't wait until I get married!" Just recently, scientists have discovered that when a man (or boy) hears a woman making sounds, such as moaning and groaning during sex, that it causes chemicals to be released in the man's brain. These chemicals cause him to get excited, which makes him be able to reach an orgasm much easier. As a young child, I didn't know exactly what my parents were doing, but I knew it was something very good the way my mother carried on and I knew it was something that married couples did. It was a very pleasant experience for me and one that made me look forward to the same thing when I grew up.

Chapter 2

The Shape of Things to Come

Shapes, we all know what shapes are; some are pleasant, some may even be disturbing. The long slender shape of a snake may cause some people to jump back in fright, even if it is not a real snake, but only something that looks like one. Other shapes seem to be pleasant to look at, like a round, smooth, brown loaf of bread. Texture and color also play a role in what looks or feels pleasant.

Anthropologists have discovered that men are attracted to the shape of a woman's breasts. This is no surprise you say; men have always known this. There is a reason, however, why men are attracted to their breasts. Of course, the obvious reason is that it excites them and makes them want to have sex, thus passing on their genes. There is more to it than that, according to those that study human behavior. Women, unlike other animals, have breasts that look engorged all the time. If you look at chimps, gorillas or monkeys, their breasts are relatively flat, even when they are nursing young. They are also covered in hair. This would not attract the male of their species very much. On the other hand, the female woman has breasts that are not covered in hair and look swollen all the time. It seems, too, the more swollen they look the more attention they get from males.

In the animal world, especially with primates, when the females are in estrous and when they are ready to conceive, their genital area swells. In some species of primates, this goes to extremes and is not only swollen to excessive size, but is also bright red. This is an advertisement to the males that they are read to mate.

In humans, there are similar dynamics at play. The large round shape of the female's breasts has been preprogrammed into the male's brain. The crack created by her cleavage or her bottom also quickly gets a man's attention. The curves of her hips and even the way they sway when she moves is hardwired into the mind of a man. Even a woman's legs attract a man attention. This is because they are smooth and taper up, getting larger towards the parts he desires. They are like runways towards the more interesting areas. The farther up he sees, the more he is attracted. It is well known that a man is visually stimulated by what he sees when he looks at a woman.

Anthropologists say that if a man is attracted to a female's body then he will stay with her after she produces his offspring. He will stay so he can continue mating with her and in this way, he will be there to protect their young.

Besides the breasts and the curves of the female's hips, there are other things that makes a man want to mate with her. Ornamentation like her long hair or even the covering between her legs gets a man's attention. Then the other visual thing and maybe the most important are the eyes. The eyes can say many things and without this look of acceptance the female gives the male, there will usually not be any sex.

For centuries, women have used make-up around their eyes to make them appear more attractive. Even animals use their eyes to communicate their intentions to others of their kind. It is not different in humans.

In today's world, there are photographs of women that men often like to look at. Men usually do not fully understand why they enjoy looking at these reflections of light off the paper. They think they just like the image they see. The truth is there is much more at play here. This is because the female image they are looking at does not run away, and she has all the shapes in the right places that he enjoys viewing. Often, these images excite him and make him want to mate. Most do not completely comprehend why they are excited when looking at the photographs of beautiful, naked women. They just think they look sexy.

One thing that most do not understand is that most of these photographs of gorgeous women have the women looking directly at the man with eyes that are speaking volumes. The eyes are saying, "Would you like to have sex with me? I am yours if you want me. Do I look good to you?" Or even, "Make love to me, now!"

Most men never stop and think about all this, they just like what they see and it is no surprise that they very much enjoy looking at the photographs. They love gazing at the image of a female because she is sending all the signals to his brain. She is signaling that she wants to have sex with him. As this is happening, he has the urges and desires programmed in his mind for certain shapes of a female's body along with the signals her eyes and expressions are sending him. All this sexual information flooding his mind can have a very strong pull on a man. Many times, a female does not have to be that attractive, but if she knows how to make a man feel wanted and accepted it will have positive results. She can do this by words, a smile, eye contact, or with a touch. She can, in this way, let him know that she can please him very much and make him glad that he's a man.

The females also have some basic instincts. As mentioned, they develop into a woman that usually wants to bear offspring. She has a little different agenda in selecting a mate than a man does, however.

Women usually are not as visually stimulated as men, but they certainly are attracted to a handsome man. What makes them attracted are similar things that attracts a man to a woman. "Is this man strong enough to mate with me successfully? Is he built right to be able to fulfill his biological purpose of fathering offspring? Will this man be a good father to our offspring?" If he is big and strong and handsome she may feel he can produce big, strong children.

He can also defend her against rival males and provide enough food for her and his offspring

This was truer in caveman times, but today it is still in in a woman's subconscious only it comes out a little differently. Today, this still might be what her internal instincts are saying to her, but she may see it a little differently. She just sees a tall, dark and handsome man that has a good-looking body and feels attracted to him physically. As in times past, she may be attracted to a man's looks, but what might be even more important is if he can provide for her and her children. This is why today many women want wealthy men for husbands.

Men want a beautiful, sexy woman to have sex with, women want a man that will romance them, hold them and make them feel secure. I once heard of an elderly lady saying, "Having a man around makes the afraid go away."

If you want to read more about selecting a mate you can read my book How to care for your M.A.N. (Mate's Animalistic Needs) or my book called I.N.S.T.I.N.C.T.S. (Interesting Natural Secret Tendencies, If Nature Could Teach Secrets) They have a great deal to say about men and women.

Chapter 3

Getting Down to the Basics

Now we move on to the basic instincts of having sex. Let's just say you have found that man or woman of your dreams. You have courted for a while and have finally said, "I do." Now what?

It might surprise many to know that there is a lot of misinformation about sex. What's worse, is that many do not know even the basics. Either they have never read about it, don't understand what they have read or they haven't been told what to expect.

I have given a lot of information so far, but not on how to have sex yet. This is coming up. I will try to give as much information that is needed. I will talk about how to have sex and how it works. You have the biological reasons why all life has sex, but now I want to delve deeper into explaining how it works and why.

I will explain in simple language and in terms that I believe will not offend anyone. If you are reading this, I believe you wish to understand maybe more than you do. If you have all the knowledge you need and know all there is to know about sex, you can skip this part and go to the next one. There I will go into the other dimensions, which will make sex even greater. Right now, however, I just want to focus on the physical aspect of how it works.

On the following pages, I will take you through this process step by step and systematically. At times, it might be humorous, but I am doing this on purpose because sex is fun. It is to be enjoyed. In addition, many a truth is said in jest. So, hang on, it will be a wild and bumpy ride!

Chapter 4

Getting in the Mood

This is the first step and sometimes, if the first step goes wrong, it can cause you not to want to even make the trip. This is because there are many misconceptions about how to get a man or woman "in the mood."

Many think you just need to kiss a few times then jump right in. This can be done, occasionally, if time is very limited or you are already in the mood, but usually it is much better to warm up the engine before racing the car.

First, let's get the woman ready, and let's for the sake of argument, say that she is a new bride and has never had sexual intercourse before. Most of this will apply even if you have been married a long time.

A woman has many places on her body that are erogenous zones. These spots or areas are extra sensitive to pleasurable sensations that will arouse her and put her 'in the mood." Most know the common ones, but I will point them out for the beginner and then mention others that may not be as well known. Usually the ones that get the most attention are the lips, then the breasts, the nipples of the breasts, the inner thighs, the butt, and of course the vagina area, especially the clitoris. Others areas that are also very pleasurable for the woman to be kissed on are the eyes, ears, or the back of the neck. Each woman is a little different and some like certain places touched or kissed more than others. Even from day to day, their preference can change. Anywhere on the body can be an erogenous zone. The feet, toes, wrists, arms, fingers, small of the back, shoulders, belly. Wow, I've just about covered the entire woman's body. That's right, it is not just the lips, breast and vaginal areas that turn them on.

Now that we know where to start, you may begin. As you kiss her mouth, you will usually feel a rush of blood surging through your sex organ. This is normal. Your organ will swell and become very stiff, rigid and hard or all of the above. This is to prepare you for the step just ahead.

After you kiss her mouth a few times, she most likely will open it more and more and want to French kiss. This is a good sign. After several passionate kisses, move down to the side of her neck, up to her eyes, or down to her breasts and give them some attention. Now, just dwell on the nipples, kiss or touch all around the breasts then keep returning to the nipple area. The woman also sometimes needs to let her husband know what she likes. Communication during this time can be very important. Let him know by making sounds that will tell him if he is in the right place. You can even move his hand or head to the places you want touched or kissed. Do not, however, be like a drill sergeant and bark out orders, (unless he happens to like that and there are some that do).

During this time of foreplay, the woman will also be going through some changes in her body that are preparing her to receive her husband inside. She will begin to produce a clear lubricant in the vaginal area. This is there for obvious reasons. Friction can be a problem if she does not have enough lubricant. If she is not turned on sufficiently, there will not be enough or if she is a more mature woman this can sometimes be a problem, too. There are lubricants on the market just for this and they should be used if needed. Some lubricants can add sensation as well.

Most of the time after the kissing and touching, the man moves his hand down to her legs. Here he can softly run his hand or hands all over her bottom and inner thighs. As he gently touches her inner thighs, he can move his hand upward, stroking the inside of her thighs up towards her vagina. Once here, he can gently find and softly touch the clitoris. This can be done slowly and teasingly also. He can move his hand close then away, building up the anticipation each time. Then when he finally reaches the most sensitive spot on her body, she will sigh with pleasure. The clitoris is usually small. It can be almost invisible or very pronounced, but either way it is full of nerves that are very sensitive.

Some women can have orgasms just by having their breasts stimulated, but this is rare. There are many, however, that cannot have an orgasm unless the clitoris is directly stimulated.

This direct stimulation can usually be achieved during intercourse if the man is in a high enough position where the penis is in contact with the clitoris as he moves back and forth. In other positions, the man can actually stimulate the clitoris with his finger while he is inside.

Since many if not most women can have and do have multiple orgasms, the man may want to stimulate the clitoris to make her reach an orgasm first and then be inside for her next one. Usually the second orgasm is about as good as the first and sometimes better. There are other ways to stimulate the clitoris which will be discussed later.

At this point, I think I should mention the "G spot". Many claim there is no such thing and some swear there is. It is like the legend of Bigfoot, some swear they have seen him and some say he is a myth. It could also be that some women have one and some do not. Many people have double the amount of taste buds on their tongue as I do, while others cannot taste seasoning as well and need more on their food. If the G spot does exist, it is somewhere towards the back of the vagina and a few inches in. If this G spot is stimulated during sexual intercourse the woman is supposed to have an explosive orgasm, so it is worth the effort to find out if she has it and make her feel as good as you can.

If the woman has not had intercourse for a long period, she may have a small vaginal opening at first. It may take several attempts for the man to get inside. The vaginal opening will have to be gently stretched to allow him to penetrate. After a few to several attempts, things should be fine. The same goes for a virgin. However, for a virgin there will usually be a little pain the first time. This is because the hymen has to be "broken". It is up to the man to do this. When he goes inside and comes to it, he should make one strong thrust to break it. Usually there is no problem, but occasionally the woman will have visit a doctor and have the doctor break it if it is thicker than normal.

Each time a couple makes love can be a little different. It's like having a taste for steak one day, chicken the next and pizza the next. Our tastes are changing all the time. Each man and woman will, however, have certain things they usually like sexually.

Now let's discuss the man. Many women, when they try to get a man turned on, just grab the genitals, fondle them a few seconds and think they are done. Sadly, some don't even do this. They see that he has an erection and assume he is ready. This might be true and work for a man in his prime who is already in the mood and ready to get down to business, but not for most men. Even if he is ready, he still likes to be touched, the same as a woman enjoys it. This is truer as a man gets older.

Men also can have just as many erogenous zones as women. Most men love to be touched by a woman and there are certain places that are their favorite. Each man, like each woman, is a little different. Some love their testicles to be touched and fondled very gently. Others like them to be gently pulled and tugged on. This, however, is not pleasant for other men and they may like something else. Some men like their nipples stimulated, with others, it has no effect on them at all. Each man will have to tell his wife what he likes and it can vary from day to day and sometimes even from minute to minute during lovemaking.

Oftentimes, women think that the penis is the only thing a man wants touched. It is true that this is the main organ they use to have sex with, but it is not the only way to stimulate him. The penis has a ring at the head that is very sensitive. The shaft also feels very pleasurable to be touched.

Most men today are circumcised, a few are not. I was born at home and was never circumcised and I have heard both sides of the argument on this. If the man stays clean, he usually will never have a problem. An uncircumcised man has more sensitivity to touch. Most do not know that when a baby boy is born, there is a thin membrane under the foreskin that protects the head of the penis. As the boy gets older, this membrane breaks and allows the skin to be pulled back all the way. Therefore, nature has designed protection for the uncircumcised male.

When the man begins to get excited the penis will swell and become very rigid. Shortly afterwards, if he stays aroused, there will be clear lubricating fluid produced.

A young man usually does not have a problem getting hard or staying that way, but as he gets older there could be issues that can cause difficulty in getting an erection and/or keeping it. Besides health issues that cause erectile dysfunction, it usually takes more stimulation for an older man to get hard and stay that way.

Many do not understand that the biggest sex organ is the brain. No matter how much stimulation there is, unless the brain is involved you will not get the results you are wanting. A man's penis is flaccid probably 97 to 98% of the time. Yes, a man can get an erection even during his sleep, and does quite often, but in order for him to perform with a woman, he has to focus and this is done by the brain. When a man is young, he will often have to get his mind off of what he is doing during sex. If he is about to reach an orgasm first and wants to reach it with his wife, he will have to think of something that has nothing to do with sex and slow down or even stop to avoid ejaculating.

As he gets older, sometimes it takes much longer for him to reach an orgasm and he will have to focus more. This can be good for the woman because she can have one or more orgasms while she is waiting for her husband to reach his first.

The male is visually stimulated and he will focus on the woman's breasts, her face, or see in his mind what he is doing with her in order to keep going up to higher plateaus until orgasm is reached. It takes less focusing for a young man, just the physical stimulation is probably enough, but as you are together longer, the brain will have to help in reaching orgasm.

Because a man is visually stimulated by looking at a woman, his wife can learn to get him in the mood by several means. Besides flirting or kissing, she can excite him by wearing something sexy around him, slowly undressing in front of him, or even dancing for him.

Many times, while one is stimulating their partner, it is a good idea for the other to be doing the same. This way, both will be ready for intercourse at the same time.

You can also use food products such as chocolate syrup or whipped cream to spice things up. Ice cubes, feathers or wearing sexy clothes such as push-up bras can make things more stimulating. Make the sexual experience fun not methodical. Some use sex toys. There is the possibility, however, that one partner could enjoy the toy more than the partner, and this could lead to jealously.

There are a few other ways of stimulating a man that we will discuss later, but now that the man has a good erection, we are ready for him to start the act of intercourse.

These are several positions that can be used and most know of a few. I will not go into every position possible because no one can do them all or want to. In addition, some may be harmful to your health or your partner's. The most well-known is the "missionary position" or the "man on top" position. This position has many advantages. Humans are about the only mammal, or for that matter, animal on earth that copulates with the male and female facing one another.

By facing one another you can kiss, look each other in the eyes and the man can use his weight to thrust. In this position, the man can also move forward slightly, thus moving the penis against the woman's clitoris for direct stimulation. Sometimes however, the clitoris is too small for this to work. Luckily, many women can have orgasms by vaginal stimulation alone. Also in this position, the man and can see and hopefully reach the woman's breasts. One last advantage is that the woman may be able to twist a little sideways and reach behind her husband to fondle his testicles as he is thrusting in and out of her, thus stimulating him even more. This also makes it a little easier for him to kiss one of the breasts as they are directly in front of him. This position only works if the woman is the correct height compared to the man and if she is limber enough.

The next common position is the "woman on top." This is popular because the woman can have some control, or complete control if she wants. Men like it because the breasts are right above them so they can easily be reached, which will stimulate them both. Additionally, in this position the man can place his hands on her bottom to get better leverage while he is thrusting. It is no accident that the palm of his hands fits perfectly around the buns of her bottom as if they were made for just such a purpose. If a woman is in her last months of pregnancy this can be a good position, too.

One gentle man that was in his late fifties complained to me once about women's breasts sagging when they aged. "Yes," I said, "but if the woman is on top of you, her breasts will hang down closer so you can reach them." He laughed and said, "Yeah I had never thought of it that way."

Some like the position of the woman on her knees with the man behind (or doggie style). This, too, is common and is a good position especially if the woman is pregnant. I have read that this position is often used if the woman is having difficulty in conceiving. One of the drawbacks to this position, however, is that you can't reach her mouth to kiss her.

There is another position that can be used if the woman is pregnant and it is also a good one even if she's not. It is the "underneath position." The woman lies on her back at a right angle to the man who is under her legs. He can then inter her from underneath. In this position, he can see her face and her breasts. He can also reach at least one of her breasts with his hand and can also reach her clitoris with his hand.

There are some positions that are good when you are young or for those couples that are at the right height or body build. Facing each other on your side with the woman's leg over top of the man so he can get inside can be good, if it will work for you. In this position, she can normally reach his testicles in order to stimulate him more during lovemaking. One of the woman's breasts is also available to kiss or touch. It is very similar to the man on top position only the couple is on their sides.

As you age or get overweight some of these positions may not work. If you get too overweight, it can be like two "Weebles" trying to mate.

Now that the man is inside, we can begin. Sometimes, however, even for the man to get inside can be an enjoyable endeavor. A man can go in only about an inch and then stop. He then can kiss, touch and stimulate the woman while he is "holding his position." A little later, he can move in another inch and repeat the process. He can continue until he is in all the way. By then the woman should be very excited.

During the sex act itself, each partner can do things that will make the other feel good either physically or emotionally. The man can get more excited if the woman talks to him, moans and groans, or touches him. The woman can call him endearing names, tell him how good it feels and let him know he is a great lover. She can also smile, use teasing gestures with facial expressions, or even push her breasts up to offer them to him. By putting her arms around his neck, she can pull him closer. By putting her hands on his hips, she can help him thrust, or by putting her hands on his chest, she can hold him up if he may be getting tired. There are many ways the woman can participate in lovemaking. There are times, too, that the man may wish her to just lie back and take it, but most of the time he would like her to help.

The man also can do several things to make sex more enjoyable for the woman. First, make sure she is ready by providing enough foreplay. When you are inside, you can tell her how sexy she is and/or how beautiful. Letting her know that she is very important to you and love her is good. Letting her tell you what she wants or likes can make things go even better. There needs to be communication before and during sex. When you are trying to make her feel good, ask her if it *is* good because you may not be hitting the right spot or making the right movements to get the result you want. Sometimes she may like for you to hold her tight, other times she may like for you to hold her arms above her head like you are ravishing her and she is helpless to stop you. Never do anything, however, that will hurt either of you physically or emotionally. There can be serious repercussions if you hurt your partner's feeling during lovemaking. Making love is the most personal thing you can do with another human being. During this time, they are very vulnerable. This is because they have to open up their heart and body to allow you in physically and emotionally. If something bad happens during this time, they may close that door and it could be difficult to open it again.

The goal, or what many think is the goal, is to reach an orgasm simultaneously. This can be a very good goal, but this often takes some time to learn how to achieve and it is not the most important thing. The most important thing is to be together enjoying one another.

Once engaged in sex, it is best to have an orgasm, however. During the sex act, tension is built up, and during orgasm, this tension is suddenly released. In a woman, there are waves that pulse through and over the vaginal wall as she experiences an orgasm.

A man produces millions of sperm a day. During sexual stimulation and/or intercourse, the tension builds until orgasm. It is then released in one explosive moment (which lasts about five to seven seconds). An orgasm in a woman lasts about nine seconds or so. When a man ejaculates, it works on the same principle as vomiting. That does not sound very romantic, but just like the waves in the esophagus, which rapidly shoves the stomach contents out, so does an ejaculation. Once the man's orgasm is over, he may feel tired and sleepy, and want to rest. It is something like the salmon that spawn. Once they fulfill their mission of reproducing themselves, they go belly up and die. This sounds a little humorous but it's true. When a man has an orgasm, it releases a tremendous amount of stress. It is like being given a sedative or a tranquilizer. Often men want to have sex just to relieve their stress. Sometimes women feel that release of stress and sometimes instead of calming them they are revved up.

This being very tired and sleepy happens more to older men than younger ones. Many times, a young man can keep going and have two or even three orgasms in a row if he is excited enough.

During copulation, a man usually has control of the process. He slows down, speeds up, has longer thrust or more shallow ones. There is a little-known fact, however, that if a man gets to the point of ejaculation and tries to go too slow, his body has an auto reflex that will take over, speed up, and begin to thrust faster. This has only rarely happened to me, but the first time it really surprised me. It's like your body says, "Hey stupid, you're not going fast enough! Here let me show you how it's done!"

Chapter 5

I Can't Get No Satisfaction!

There are several reasons one or the other may not have an orgasm during sexual intercourse. Problems at work, the children sick, overwhelming debt weighing on a person's mind are some. There could be health problems, either temporary or permanent.

As men get older, their hormone production diminishes. Besides this, they can sometimes have problems staying erect and this can be caused by the things above or by medical problems. Women's hormone levels go down during and after menopause, which will affect her desire too.

Therefore, during sex, one of the partners may reach an orgasm first and the other may fail to achieve it. This can be a problem for either one. They may feel left out. If they feel left out they may feel that the other doesn't love them or care if they felt good or not. Sex is supposed to be good. It is supposed to bond each other together in body and mind, but if there is a problem in the bedroom, it can cause more problems outside its doors.

First, if the woman cannot achieve an orgasm during sexual intercourse it is the duty of her husband to make it happen afterwards if necessary. Women sometimes just enjoy the closest of her husband loving on her and an orgasm may not be as important to them. They should tell you if they need to reach an orgasm if they didn't achieve one with you. If the wife has a problem reaching orgasms during normal sex, it would probably be better for her husband to make her reach it before they have intercourse.

This is because he may become sleepy and want to rest after he is finished, leaving her frustrated.

Men's goal is usually to have an orgasm during sex, so if the wife has an orgasm or several and he fails to get one he will probably feel left out. He could also feel like a failure, less than a man, unable to fulfill his husbandly duties and unable to please his wife. Men may look big and strong but their egos are often very fragile.

Most women want romance instead of raw, hot sex (there always exceptions and things can change from day to day). Men are turned on by what they see and women are turned on more of what they feel. Men's sex organs are on the outside of their bodies and women's are on the inside. This is true of the way they often view sex. Men look at the outside of a woman's body and are turned on and women internalize their emotions in order to desire sex from a man.

Each one needs to understand the other's needs. Many women want romance while their husband just wants sex. Their man is turned on and his hormones are raging and he just wants to take his wife to the bedroom and ravish her.

Men sometimes forget that the woman wants to be loved and cherished, not just used as a release for their pent up sexual frustrations. So, each one needs to be aware of the other's needs. If the woman gives her husband raw sex and satisfies him, he is much more apt to shower her with affection and love. If the husband shows his wife love and kindness, she is more apt to give him good hot sex.

This is a good time to say that sex should never, ever be used as a weapon. Many women use it to try to control their husbands and vice versa. This can do a lot more damage than many realize. If your mate is faithful, they have no one else to go to that will fulfill their sexual needs. If this continues, they will feel they are not loved, and if another someone else gives them any attention at all they may be very tempted to find comfort in their arms instead of yours.

Now back to making your spouse have an orgasm if they failed to achieve one during lovemaking. There are other ways to make each other reach an orgasm if they fail to do so during normal intercourse. If the woman needs direct stimulation, her husband can do so with his finger, while he is kissing her or touching her elsewhere. He can also use the tip of his penis to directly stimulate the clitoris. Sometimes, the woman would like to do the stimulating herself, while her husband kisses or touches her on one or more of her erogenous zones.

Likewise, if the man needs stimulation because he failed to reach an orgasm, his wife can provide it. She can directly stimulate his sex organs by fondling and masturbating him. This can be done while he is watching her. Since men are visually stimulated, she can be in a position where he can watch her please him. This can be her in a sitting position so he can focus on her breasts and face, or she can lie down and open her legs so he can see more of her womanly charms. She can also lie in his arms above him so she can kiss him while he masturbates. In this position, she can fondle his testicles and inner thighs, while he can touch her bottom and see and/or feel her breasts on his chest. She can also take over masturbating him if he gets tired.

One other way is for her to be on her knees above him. He can masturbate while she fondles his testicles. In this position, he can kiss her mouth and/or her breasts. He can also fondle her breasts with his free hand.

When your partner touches you, and pleases you sexually while they are only enjoying it emotionally it makes you feel as if they truly love you. When a man makes love to a woman, she can actually lie there and receive pleasure without participating, but when a woman pleases her husband by masturbating him and making him reach an orgasm with her own hands he feels she is actually making love to him. This not only makes him feel good physically, it is very good emotionally.

How often is often enough? This will vary from couple to couple and from person to person. Some men, when they are young and in their prime, want sex every day. Others may be satisfied by having it only a couple of times a week. When I say sex, it can mean having intercourse with their wife or just needing to have an orgasm. A women's sexual appetite can vary quite a bit, too. As couples age, things can and will change.

Sometimes there are conflicts in the amount of sex one or the other wants or needs. This can be a big issue. There needs to be compromise so you can meet somewhere in the middle. Each partner should be aware and concerned about the other's needs and wants and try to fulfill them unless they are unreasonable. Some may think, especially when they get older, that their desire has left. Many times, desire fades, but if you start kissing and "fooling around" it will trigger that desire and sex can be great. Often times when you don't seem to be in the mood or even thinking about sex, but end up having it, the orgasms will be terrific. Other times when you are "horny" and have sex, the orgasm will be just good, but not great.

Many may be thinking, what about oral sex? I am saving this for last. Some do not practice oral sex for several reasons. It repulses many women and even some men. There are several reasons for this. First, I should say that one thing that repulses women is that they think it is "dirty". This can be true, if the man does not bathe enough. Most sex should be done after bathing for obvious reasons. You should always think of your partner. They do not want to smell your body odor. They want you to be desirable and welcoming, not repulsive. There can be times when a spontaneous moment arrives where even a quick shower may spoil the moment. At these times, you will have to take things as they are and enjoy one another. Most often, however, there will be time to prepare.

Many men like to receive oral sex, but they do not like to give it. Some like to give and receive. Many women like to give it more than they like to receive it, and others, just as men do, enjoy giving and receiving. I am not going to say one way or the other that oral sex should be done or not be done. It is up to each couple to decide. I often look to nature to get an answer. No animal actually engages in oral sex to make his or her mate reach an orgasm. Some male animals will momentary lick the female just before hopping on, so there is some "oral sex". There are also several degrees of oral sex. There can be just a little to get the man or woman in the mood, or there can be more. My thinking, and this is solely my opinion, there is nothing wrong with kissing and stimulating each other orally. I have no problem with a man bringing the woman to orgasm orally by clitoral stimulation. I also believe oral sex to bring a man to orgasm is fine, if the woman does not take the sperm into her mouth. The vagina was made for a man to ejaculate his sperm in, not a woman's mouth. I believe that he should not use her to fulfill his needs in that way.

This is my thought on the subject. If neither the husband nor wife feels comfortable giving or receiving oral sex, they should not do it. If they enjoy it, it is up to them. Therefore, if both husband and wife have no problem with it, I cannot say it is wrong.

There is one thing I will interject at this point and that is anal sex. A few couples engage in it and I have to again go to nature to tell you that it is not natural. No animal in the entire world has anal sex. The female is designed specifically for the penis of the male. The double-headed opossum's penis is made especially for the double womb female. The corkscrew penis of a Muscovy duck is made just for the hen. The six-foot long penis of the elephant is designed to reach the female as he mounts her. Likewise, the human penis is designed to fit perfectly into the vagina of the woman.

During anal sex, the woman can be injured because the rectum is not designed for her husband to be inside. It can tear and bleed and be very painful. There is no natural lubricant produced as in the vagina. There also can be harmful bacterial, which can be transferred to the vagina, so anal sex is defiantly not natural.

In nature, there are no "factory recalls", because everything in nature is designed perfectly for the purpose it is used for.

Part 4:
The Fourth Dimension of Sex

Love is the fourth dimension. Sadly, some never find or possess real love. Many believe so, but never let go and give totally of themselves. In this forth part I will talk about love and why it is important to have while engaging in sex. Many today think sex is just for pleasure, but without love, they are missing the best part of sex.

Chapter 1

Finding Love

In today's world, love is seldom fully appreciated. Many talk about having sex as "making love." That can be true, but it also can be very false. You should never have sex without loving the person. I will explain why in more detail. This might sound old fashion but men and women have been here a long time, over many centuries, and the family unit has kept civilization intact.

In a relationship between a man and woman, there can be and are many variables. Some things, however, are common in almost all relationships. This was true long ago and it is still true today.

I will explain why marriage is important later, but right now, I would like to say something about commitment. First, I will say something about how women look at it. It seems that deep down in a woman's psyche there is a need for her man to be committed to her. This is an innate feeling, which has caused women to be a one-man woman for centuries. Today it is not easy to find a man who will make a life-long commitment. I will discuss why later. Because of the great number men not wanting to make a commitment, many women give themselves sexually to a man they care for or love. They hope by doing so the man will want them, fall in love and want to make that commitment and marry them. This does not always work. There is an old saying and it is true, "Why buy the cow when the milk is free?"

If it is a kind of man that is afraid of commitment or just does not want to make one, he is more likely than not, to never make it. If the man *truly loves* the woman, he *will* make a commitment and he will marry her.

There are women the same way. They may have been hurt in the past and afraid that this man, too, will stop loving her and walk out of her life. Because of this, she may never truly give her entire heart to him.

Most think that men are tougher than women are, are less emotional, and do not feel the pain as much as women do when they are hurt. On the contrary, men that have been badly hurt by a woman may be terrified of commitment or may not want to give a woman their heart again.

As I explained in earlier chapters, sex is for reproducing one's self or one's own kind. This is just the biological reason for sex, but there is much more. Once you do bring a child into the world you will have to raise it until that child is old enough to make it on its own. While you are raising your offspring, more than likely you will acquire one or two more. You will then have to protect them, feed them, clothe them and educate them.

It will take many years of time, effort and hard work to achieve this rearing of children. In order for you to do this, you will have to be with them. Some today do not think this is necessary, but in the human species, it is natural for both parents to be involved in raising the young. The way God designed the human species is that he made them certain ways, which will keep the family unit together. The anthropologist's view is that the male will stay with a female so he will be able to mate with her. While the male is hanging around waiting to mate with the female (when she will let him), he becomes bored. He then goes out with the boys and hunts wild game. The female and young get the food he brings home, which makes his mate happy so she lets him mate with her again and again.

This is said in jest, but much of it is true. This is how many animals do it, but humans have a different dimension that keeps them together and that is love.

Without love, sex is just a physical act. It is very pleasurable either way, but with love, it has a much deeper meaning. When a man and woman marry, they forsake all others for that one special person. This bond is supposed to guarantee to the man that he will always have a sexual partner. It is also supposed to guarantee to the woman that she will have someone beside her who will protect her, feed her and help care for the young.

Love is the glue that holds the family unit together. At least it should be. Today some marriages are held together for conveniences sake, for love of money, or from fear. The fear can be for several different reasons that are too numerous to go into.

Love is not *just* an emotional feeling although it can be and is. When a man and woman meet and there is chemistry between them there are actually chemicals released in their brains. These chemicals make them happy and feel euphoric. This "natural high", however, wears off in about six months. After this period, you may wake up one morning beside this man or woman that you have committed the rest of your life to, look over at them lying next to you asleep with drool coming out of their mouth, hair disheveled, and you think, "Oh Lord, what have I done?"

This is natural and may happen. The one you chose is not a prince or princess. They are not a god or goddess, but a human being. They have flaws and faults just like every other man or woman on earth. They don't always look their best, they smell when they sweat, they stink when they pass gas and they vomit when they get sick.

Love looks past this and sees the good things that caused you to fall in love with them. They see the same bad things in you, and you hope that they, too, will look past your flaws and faults and see what's on the inside.

There are also many kinds of love: The love you have for your children, the love you have for your father or mother, the love you have for your brothers and sisters or the love you have for your spouse. This love for your spouse is supposed to be the greatest of all human love. You are to forsake all others, if necessary, for that person.

When you come together as a husband and wife, there is bound to be things that will cause strife. Things will not always go smooth. Love is like a living, breathing plant or animal. It needs care or it will become weak, wither and die. It takes two to make love work like it is supposed to, but it only takes one to destroy it. You can love someone with all your heart, you can even die for them, but if they don't return that love it is in vain.

In a marriage, you must definitely live by the Golden Rule; do unto your spouse as you would have them do unto you. Never, ever, lie to one another. A marriage is based on trust—and above all, never, ever, be unfaithful!

Do not let jealously destroy a good relationship. Falsely accusing your spouse of being unfaithful destroys many marriages. When there are disagreements, you need to fight fair. Do not say things that are untrue just to get back at them. You cannot call words back. Don't say "you always" or "you never" when in a verbal disagreement with your spouse.

Many times, a little derogatory comment can get quickly out of hand. A snide remark that hurts the one can cause them to say something back that will hurt the other. Soon the person that is hurt will say something even more hurtful because he or she wants the one hurting them to stop doing it. This does not work because it is like trying to put fire out with fire. Remember, "A soft answer turns away wrath, but grievous words stir up anger."

We all need to stop and think about what we say and do. When we are young, we often take it for granted that our mate will always be beside us. This is not true. There will always come a day that you will lose them, for one of you will die. Unfortunate today, with divorce rates at 50% or more, your marriage may not last the test of time. I have lost one wife that I loved by divorce and another by death. No matter the reason, when you lose someone you love, it hurts. They are not there beside you anymore. You cannot touch them, hold them or even talk to them. Their love for you is gone forever. You are alone and the emptiness inside is worse than a great sickness. The faults and flaws they had no longer matter. You would take all their faults and more if you could once again have them beside you. You miss the look in their eyes when you gazed into them. You miss the gentle touch they often gave you. You miss the sound of their voice and the words, "I love you." You also miss their laughter and their expressions. The little things they would say or do that endeared you to them. Yes, love is the greatest thing on earth and without it, your marriage is not a marriage, it is just two people existing together. Without love, marriage will never be what it should be. Nevertheless, even if you don't have love in your marriage, it can be found because love comes from the heart. You must open your heart or love cannot enter. Many today have closed their hearts because of hurt, fear or some other reason, but it can be reversed.

In the last section of the book, I will show you another dimension of sex, the fifth dimension. It will show you a deeper love and the true reason sex is good.

Chapter 2

What's Love Got to do With It?

Love has everything to do with a serious relationship and a marriage, which is the most serious relationship of all. Without love, all you have during sex is animal lust and desires.

Few creatures in the animal kingdom bond together for life. A few long-lived birds do but almost no other mammal besides man does. Primates usually have several females in which to mate with. The male and female human bond is probably stronger than any in the animal kingdom. This bond is called love. It is given to man, both male and female, for a reason. Human civilization could not be what it is without this bond. If we were like most other animals, the males would constantly be fighting over females and there would be little time for anything else.

Almost all higher mammals come into estrus only once a year and some like the elephant, do only every few years. Males do not have a chance to mate very often. With humans, the female can have sex nearly all the time. This is a big reason for the male to be near and to protect the female. Being around the female to protect her from other males, which want to have sex with her, is called "mate guarding." I will speak about it in a later chapter.

Love is the substance that keeps men and women together or should keep them together. Love is the greatest gift man has, for no other creature on earth has it. This is what sets humans apart from all other life forms. If there would be no love in the world, man would be just like any other predatory animal. Let us hope love will never die, because if it does, all of humanity will die with it.

Chapter 3

Poem: What is Love?

Next are a few poems. I wrote the first one recently for this book. The next two are from my wife that passed away suddenly and unexpectedly, and the last ones I wrote to my wife Lilly.

What is love?

Love is something that you cannot pick up and hold in your hand. / It is invisible to the naked eye and cannot be seen by mortal man.

Love is like the wind that comes then softly and gently blows, / drifting slowly past until it fades and gradually goes.

Its substance cannot be seen, touched, smelled or even heard, / yet the evidence of it cannot even be put into a thousand words.

It can be felt, not only in our mind, but also in our heart. / It is strong when we are together; it is even stronger when we are apart.

Love is what keeps the world turning and all the evil at bay. / It's what makes life worth living each and every day

It is stronger than anger, hate or any other thing. / For only with love, can true happiness bring.

This is only the beginning of the description of love. / Yes, it is the greatest of all gifts and it comes from God up above.

I also read once that love is never boastful, never selfish, never prideful and always willing to forgive. Love is the greatest thing on earth. It is also the greatest thing in heaven for *God is love,* 1 John 4:8 and 4:16.

Chapter 4

Love for a Husband

This next poem and the letter that follows is what my late wife, Elizabeth, wrote to me. The letter was for one of our anniversaries. She had a way of putting into words what she felt in her heart.

Elizabeth's Poem

Dreams don't come true; I gave up long ago.
I was longing for someone I knew, someone I never thought I'd find. / Then I met you, and I looked in your eyes.
It was then I knew——I knew you were the one I thought I'd never find.
As I fell in love with you, I discovered the man my soul yearned for. / You were all I could possibly want and more than I had hoped for.
I saw such tenderness in your heart; I could see the kindness in your eyes. / I felt softness in your touch and love in your soul.
I yearned for a companion, a partner, a best friend and a lover. I found all this in you. / You've brought me so much joy and happiness. My life has new meaning and love like I've never known.
I promise to love you, shower you with kindness, hold you and keep you. / I'd give my life for you, for I will love you till the day I die, because you are the love of my life.

Elizabeth kept her word, for she loved me until the day she died. Her words about dying for me were also prophetic. Her death saved my life, because I nearly died from the same thing that took her.

This is the anniversary letter:

Elizabeth's Letter

I so much enjoy touching you and caressing you. I look forward to coming home. I can't describe how much I love waking up next to you. I've always thought I knew what love was, but then, I met you and love became what it should be. It changes you forever. You do what's best for your mate. You put him first; yourself last. You strive to find more ways to please your man. Your body comes alive. Joy floods your soul; peace and contentment wraps itself around you like a silk gown. Every day seems beautiful. Happiness warms your heart, and if we happen to be real lucky, we end up with a best friend, a lover, a companion and more joy and happiness than you've ever known.

Happy Anniversary Honey!
I love you beyond words and pray we have 50 more anniversaries together.

Chapter 5

Love for a Wife

The next four poems I wrote for my wife, Lilly, before we married. I almost did not put them in the book because I don't think they are very good, but she likes them and wanted them here. The last poem called *The Price of You* I wrote many years ago, and it is one of my favorites. I hope you like it.

A Treasure

A man once found a great treasure of which no one else knew. / Like him, I found a great treasure, and that great treasure was you.

Selling all he had the man bought the field so the treasure would forever be his own. / Like that man, I'm forsaking all, to have my treasure, the greatest treasure I've ever known.

When I found you my love, I found what I'd searched for, for all of my life. / A woman who'd love me with all of her heart and love being my wife.

You're a gift from heaven and I'll treat you that way forever more. / Our lives and our love are just the beginning, for there is much more in store.

Yes, you are a great treasure and I will forever thank the Lord up above. / You are my treasure sweetheart and the one I will forever love.

Written November 15, 2011

Chapter 6

My Dearest

You say that I am your dearest and I know you are my sweetheart. / When we're together we are very happy, but we're not when we're apart.

I believe in my heart that you were sent to me by the Lord up above. / For they there so many things about you that I love.

I love your eyes, your lips, your touch and your warm embrace. / I love to hear your voice and see the joy that's on your face

Yes, I can see all the love in your eyes that you have for me. / I can feel that love when I'm in your arms, and in your arms, is where I love to be.

Sweetheart, I get lost in your eyes when I'm holding you in my arms. / And I want to keep you forever there where you'll be safe from all harm.

I know beyond a doubt that I want you, need you, and will forever love you, too. / And I hope you'll be with me everywhere I go and in everything that I do

Because you, sweetheart, will be my love for the rest of my life. / If you will only say yes, and forever be my wife?

Chapter 7

Will you?

Since I met you, you've brought so much joy and happiness into my life. / Now I want you to be beside me forever. I want you, Lilly, to be my wife.

I know for sure that you were sent to me by the Lord up above. / Because no one but God could have found someone like you for me to love.

I want you next to my heart and I want you there to forever stay. / For I love you sweetheart and I will all of my days.

So please take my hand, my heart, my love and forever be in my life. / Please say you will marry me and be my loving wife.

Chapter 8

An Angel that came to Me

This is written for an angel that came to me out of the blue. / It's written from my heart and these words my love, are written just for you.

I want you to give me all of your troubles and all of your cares. / And I will hold you next to my heart and will forever keep you there.

So, lay all your burdens on my shoulders; they're strong and will always be. / For as your husband, I will be there any time, day or night, that you need me.

Please give me all of your love and all of your heart. / And I will forever give you mine, unto death do us part.

I'll give you not only my love; I'll give you my mind and my body too. / For no one deserves more love in their life, sweetheart, than you.

I'll also give you more joy, contentment and every ounce of my love. / For I know you have been sent to me by the Lord up above.

Today I take you to be my love, my joy, my happiness and I will forever be in your life. / I will always love you, sweetheart, for you are now a part of me; you are now my wife.

I LOVE YOU!

Chapter 9

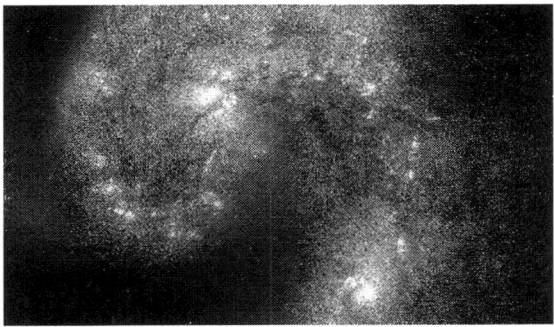

The Price of You

Who can find a virtuous woman? Her price is above any treasure I could buy. / You're a gift from God. And your price? I cannot count that high.

For if God gave me all the stars in heaven as a trade for you. / If he gave me the sun, the moon, and the earth, it still would not do.

If he gave me all the silver and gold that has ever been found. / Or the songs of all the birds; your voice has a sweeter sound.

And if I could number every grain of sand that is in the sea. / Then maybe I could begin to count all you mean to me.

For if I knew every star by name that God has hung in the sky. / Then just maybe I could begin to tell you why:

Why I love you the way that I do. / And what you're worth, for I cannot count the price of you.

Chapter 10

What is a Wife?

Here is an excerpt from my booklet called *Instruction Manual for the W.I.F.E.* because I believe it says what a wife is: In closing I will say that there may be days that you will wonder, "Why did I ever bring this woman home in the first place?" But then again, there will be times that you realize it was the smartest thing you ever did. This is because she will share all of your joys, triumphs, hopes and dreams, as well as your defeats, failures, and heartaches. She was made to share these things with you; to help you through the bad times, and to rejoice with you during the good. The woman is your companion when you're lonely; your sunshine on dark and cloudy days. She's your joy when you're sad; happiness when you're grieving; pride when you feel worthless; warmth when you're cold and comfort when you're sick. She is faithful when no one has faith in you; your help when no one will lend a hand; your understanding partner when you're not understood; and your love when others hate you. She is your everything!

She is not only your friend when you have none; she is your soul mate; your lover; and the one who chose you above all others. She was created just for you and you alone. For she is *"bone of your bone, and flesh of your flesh"*, she is a part of you! This beautiful WOMAN; the Wondrous One, Man Always Needs, is your WIFE; the Wonderful Idea from Eden!

Part 5:
The Fifth Dimension of Sex

Sometimes in our day-to-day life, we go back and forth from one dimension to the other while we are engaged with our spouse in an intimate way. One day you could want to have sex in the third dimension, while they are in the fourth. You want hot sex and they want to be loved tenderly and affectionately. Another time, it could be the other way around. Being in an adjacent dimension is not too bad as long as your partner is in the one beside you. When you are two or more dimensions apart, it can be a problem. If you only see sex as an animalistic act and they see it in the highest dimension there could be conflict. Even worse, is if they only see sex as a biological act to become pregnant and do not want to engage in it any other time and you see it as a way to express love and affection, the marriage will probably not survive.

This is another reason that I wanted to write this book, especially this last part, which shows that sex is much more than something to have just to perpetuate your species. It is more than an act that is enjoyable. It is even more than something you do to show the one you love how much you love them.

In the first dimension, we have viewed sex as just a biological act. In the second, we have seen it as something we want and have had a taste of its strong pull on our mind and body. In the third dimension, we have engaged in its thrills and pleasures and found out how good it feels physically. The forth level, is viewed through loving eyes, where it is not only seen as something that brings great pleasure to the body but also to the heart and mind.

So now, we come to the last dimension. It is the highest dimension of sex and most never achieve it. This is because they do not understand what sex is meant to convey. Sex is more than just a physical act it, is an emotional act. Sex was designed to bond two people together. Often people think they can have sex without emotional ties, but this usually doesn't happen. When a person engages in sex, they create a bond and share something more personal than any other thing they can share.

Sex is even more than a physical and emotional act it has an even deeper meaning and purpose. Therefore, in this last section of the book, I hope I can show you mysteries that you have never understood before. I will also explain what and why there is more to sex than meets the eye, much more.

Chapter 1

What is the Fifth Dimension of Sex?

This is the last and most important dimension of all. This is because it is not just a physical union of two bodies. It is not because it is the most pleasurable feeling a human body or mind can experience. It is not an act that is only to reproduce one's self. It is not even only an act that shows the other your love towards them. This is because sexual intercourse can be and is on a higher level or dimension than anything else on earth. It is because it is spiritual one.

Why spiritual? God is the one that created sex. He designed every bird, animal and creature on the earth and programmed them to be able to reproduce. All their instincts are there so they will know what to do. Humans have very similar urges, as do all other animals. Yes, we are made from the same dust as the animals, but we were created in the image of God. God is the one that invented sex. God also is the one who invented marriage. Very few birds and animals are monogamous. Most birds and animals mate with any they come across and as many as they can, so they will pass on their genes to the next generation. Often, the males will die in the endeavor and conquest of trying to win a mate.

Many of the things I have already discussed will be touched upon again, but now with a look at them through the eyes of the One who designed them.

God is not a prude. If you think so, read The *Song of Solomon*. In this Holy Scripture, it talks about the woman's breasts being like clusters of grapes, her thighs as smooth jewels and her lips having the taste of apples. It also talks about making love with her all night!

In Gen. 1:27 it says that He made them "male and female". Then He told them (in verse 28) to, "Be fruitful and multiply and replenish the earth. So here, God tells the man and his wife to have sex.

Some think that the "great sin" was when Adam and Eve had sex. This couldn't be further from the truth. They were already told to have sex and "they were both naked and were not ashamed," Gen 1:25. The sin in the Garden of Eden definitely had something to do with sex because they covered themselves afterwards, but it was not because they had sexual relations with one another. They were married and unashamed. There are several possibilities and I discuss them in the commentary of my book *CHRIST: His Words, His Life.*

How can a 'spiritual" dimension make your sex life better? When you understand the spiritual aspect of sex, you will have the deeper meaning of what sex is all about.

We can never achieve the highest pinnacle of spiritual love, at least not in this world, but you can understand it.

Chapter 2

The Beginning of Sex

We will first go back to the beginning so that we will understand how great sex was at first and then see what we are missing now.

When God first made man, He said that it was *not good* that the man should be alone. He then caused the man to fall into a deep sleep, like being given anesthesia today. He then took a rib of the man and fashioned a woman from him (think cloning). By doing this, he took one and made two. When God brought the woman to Adam, Adam said, "This is now bone of my bone and flesh of my flesh."

Right afterwards God said, "Therefore a man shall leave his father and his mother and shall "cleave unto" (have sexual intercourse with) his wife and they shall be one flesh."

The Lord also said in Mark 10:8 "And the two shall be one flesh, so then they are no more two, but one flesh." The two shall be one. This happens when they are joined together sexually.

After he created them, they were naked and were not ashamed. They had no hang-ups, no excess baggage, no misinformation about sex and no bad experiences. They were both virgins and they had no preconceived ideas about anything being bad about sex. Sex was not bad, it was good and God said that His creation was "very good."

Therefore, when Adam and Eve came together in a sexual union they were pure. They had no jealousy because of a former boyfriend or girlfriend the other had previously, and they had no resentment toward one another. They did not covet another's husband or wife because they were the only ones there. There was also no pressure about anything. There was no pressure to have a perfect sexual performance, and no worries about someone coming upon them and embarrassing them while they were making love. They also did not have to worry about going to work the next day, paying the bills, getting sick or taking care of the baby. You get what I mean. They were totally and completely free from anything that would put a damper on their intimacy.

Today, every one of these things I mentioned, plus a whole lot more, can interfere with the closeness we feel towards our sexual partner. Sickness, worry, stress, jealousy, resentment, old hurts, mistrust, fatigue, and others can take a lot of the pleasure out of sex. This is if we have sex, because often times these things can prevent couples from even engaging in intimacy.

I have written this book to help couples find not only sexual fulfillment in their marriage but to get back that connection that they have with the Creator of all things.

In this part of the book, I need to stress that to have this spiritual dimension of sex you must be married.

I know some will say that is not so, but I can prove you are wrong. I once had had a young man that I love, say to me that marriage, "is just a piece of paper."

A ten-million-dollar check is "just a piece of paper." A contract "is just a piece of paper." A summons to court "is just a piece of paper" or a warrant for your arrest "is just a piece of paper." It's what's on that paper that matters. A marriage certificate is on *just a piece of paper*, but what it says are words that state, "These two people are one." They are one in the eyes of God and they are one in the eyes of the world. They have forsaken all others to be together. They will stay together during good times and bad, during sickness and health. They will be faithful to one another until one of them draws their last breath. Yes, it is not just a piece of paper. That's why they are called marriage "vows" and not marriage "maybes". You pledge your life and heart to another person. You vow to not only them but to God that you will be with them through thick and thin, not just when you feel like it. The young man that I spoke of that thought marriage was "just a piece of paper" never had the chance to make that decision later. Soon after he said this, he was stricken with a crippling disease and now he can never be married.

Chapter 3

God Commands Us to Have Sex

Some may find this surprising. Does God really command us to have sex?

Yes, He most certainly does. When He made the first man and woman and joined them in marriage, He told them to reproduce. You must have sex to do this. He also said that the two shall no more be two, but one flesh. When they were married, and consummated that marriage with sexual intercourse, they became one. He also said, "What God has joined together let no man put asunder." Yes, God commands married couples to have sex. He limits sexual intercourse only in the bounds of marriage and He has very good reasons for this that I will speak about later. For the Bible says in Hebrews 13:4, "Marriage is honorable in all and the bed undefiled."

Also in the New Testament, the Apostle Paul says that men and woman that are married should not be apart sexually for long periods. In 1 Cor.7:3 he says, "Let the husband render unto the wife due benevolence: and likewise, also the wife unto the husband." This means you have an obligation to provide sexual affection towards your spouse. The next verse says that you do not have the right to withhold sex because your body is no longer just yours, but it also belongs to your spouse.

Chapter 4

Why Marriage?

Why is marriage important? What are the benefits of marriage? It should be obvious, but in today's world, it seems nothing is simple for many to understand. According to studies, married couples live longer. This is because of several reasons. One is that they share each other's antibodies making their immune systems stronger. Two it is that there is less stress financially because two can pay the bills better than one. Stress is also lessened emotional (if they have a good mate) because they have each other to lean on during difficult times. Third is that they have a release for their sexual needs, which also lessens emotional stress. Even sex itself is healthy. It gets the heart rate up and burns calories. It strengthens muscles, and in men, it is healthy for the prostate gland because an active sex life can help prevent prostate cancer. This is just some of the physical and emotional benefits of marriage as there is much more.

Marriage is the oldest institution there is. This is because God knew that marriage is the glue that holds civilizations together. In addition, it is love that holds the marriage together.

Every child born deserves to have and know its mother and father. This is not only a biological fact of nature it is a moral right. In nature, different species have different social lives and interactions with one another. Many birds, like chickens and other gallinaceous birds, hatch offspring that can (in a matter of hours) run and help find their own food. In this case, only the mother helps them find food, keeps them warm and protects them from danger. In other birds and animals, the males help do the protecting and sometimes the feeding. The same goes for humans. Throughout history and before, the male provided food, shelter, and protection for his offspring.

These birds and animals only care for their young for a relatively short time compared to the length humans take care of theirs. Even the long-lived animals protect and provide for their young for less than ten years and most do not do it that long. The elephant lives about as long as people and they care for their offspring nearly as long as we do. Creatures that have long lifespans must invest several years in raising their young until the young can provide for themselves. In each animal society that does so, there are rules and usually a hierarchy. This is so the next generation can continue in doing what has worked for their survival for countless centuries. Humans, today, seem to think that they know better than nature. Nature was created by God and He is wiser than any of us will ever be.

He said that sex is to be used in marriage for reproduction and to bond the two together. If we view sex with the purpose God intended, we can see it in this fifth dimension. There is something mysterious about sex that only God can see. When we are married, He sees one person! When the Lord was on the earth, He said that, "The Father and I are One." It is called an Echad and it is spiritual terminology. It means two or more that are one. "In the beginning was the Word and the Word was with God and the Word was God." John 1:1.

This spiritual mystery even goes further. God compares His people as a "bride", His bride. "He is coming for a church without a spot, wrinkle or blemish." Just as a man is supposed to take care of his wife, feed her, clothe her, protect her and yes, even be one with her, Christ will do the same in a spiritual way with His "wife." I hope you are beginning to see the correlation between a husband and wife in marriage. A marriage is a contract and both parties are supposed to be bound to that contract until one dies. When Christ takes His bride as His wife, he will make a contract and since neither He nor his wife will ever die, they will be joined forever. Now in the time of Christ and before, there was a period of betrothal or in today's terminology an engagement period. If we are followers of Christ, then we are betrothed or engaged to Him. When He returns to get His bride, we will be married. This is in Rev. 19:7-9, Rev. 21:2, Rev. 21:9 and Rev. 22:17.

This union of Christ and His church is a spiritual analogy that parallels a marriage between a man and a woman. When Christ died on the cross, blood and water came out of His side. Out of man's side came the woman, Adam's wife. Adam was an earthly man, who brought death to all. Christ is a "spiritual Adam" who brought everlasting life to all who follow him. Out of Christ's side came forth blood, which brought forth His spiritual wife, His church.

Adam was created a perfect physical man, but later he fell and caused sin to come into the world, which caused death to come to all. Christ also was a perfect physical man, but one who did not sin, and by giving His sinless life He gave back to man what he had lost. Now all those that believe and follow Him can have eternal life. This way, the "second Adam" undid what the first Adam had done.

Now you can begin to see how God views marriage. When a man and woman marry, they forsake all others. When we come to God, we are to forsake all other gods. "You shall have no other gods before me," He says. When they are married, they become one flesh. "The Father and I are one," Christ said. They are one in spirit.

A husband is supposed to love his wife so much that he will "give himself for her." Eph. 5:25 "Husbands love your wives, even as Christ also loved the church and gave himself for it."

Many do not realize what God is doing. By His church, His "wife", He is reproducing Himself. We are his children and joint-heirs with Christ, Romans 8:17. We are the sons of God, and we were made in His image

God's great plan is to reproduce Himself through us frail human beings. Most do not fully understand this. The Lord told Nicodemus that you must be born again. If we are His, He puts his spirit in us; then we are begotten. It is something like a father's sperm fertilizing an egg of the mother then the embryo begins to develop. When it is "born", it comes out a spirit being instead of an earthy one. Peter explains it clearly in 1 Peter 1:23, "Being born again, not of corruptible seed (sperm) but of incorruptible, by the word of God." This is why He told Nicodemus that, "flesh and blood cannot inherit the kingdom of God." When we are resurrected, we will be like Christ and have a spiritual body, one that will never grow old and die. In 1 Corinthians: 15:53 it says, "For this corruptible must put on incorruption and this mortal must put on immortality."

I hope you are beginning to grasp why sex and marriage is so important, so "Holy." It is not called "Holy matrimony" for nothing. Holy means to be "set apart," set apart for a specific purpose. Holy also means kadosh in Hebrew or kosher, as most know it.

Marriage and sex are a mirror image or reflection of how God is carrying out His purpose for humanity. That is why it is such a great sin if we misuse sex and take marriage lightly. If we have sex outside of marriage by joining ourselves to someone that we do not love and with one we don't have that "forever commitment" to, it degrades God's great institution. Because when a man and woman join in the sexual union, they are becoming one with each other.

God wants the best for us. He wants the best for our children. We are His creation and He wrote The Book on how we are to conduct our lives so we will be the happiest.

Yes, you can have sex outside of marriage. You can have it with many different partners and it may feel very good. God says that "there is pleasure in sin for a season."

For a while, you might really enjoy all the thrill of having multiple partners. Someday, however, it will change. In Proverbs 9:17 it says, "Stolen waters are sweet, and bread eaten in secret is pleasant." This is talking about stealing another's husband or wife and having sex in secret.

If you are a person with a conscious, then having sex just for the thrill and physical pleasure will not fulfill the deep emotional need that we all have. Casual sex is very shallow. All you are doing is scratching the surface of the meaning of love and sex. Yes, there are times a husband and wife can just let their sexual hunger go and enjoy themselves with each other. They know, however, that when it is over the other will be there for them. There is a deep emotional need in most of us for love. Not the shallow physical type, but a deep, abiding love. The kind of love that can only come from someone that loves you enough to forsake all others forever. One that will give unto you, and only unto you, all their love and physical attention. A man or woman that will stick by you through thick and thin, through better or worse, for richer or poorer and in sickness and in health until death do you part.

Chapter 5

How Can You Have This Special Love?

God's word has the answer for every aspect of our lives. I have read many articles and watched dozens of programs about the marital difficulties couples have and how it affects their sex life. I have been married for a combined total of more than forty years and to more than one woman (but only one at a time and all legally). Therefore, I have much experience in marital relationships. I have also spent hundreds of hours with over three hundred women speaking about relationships and the problems associated in them. I have heard the advice given to couples by counselors or therapists, and many times, it is the same advice the Bible gives. This is because the truth works no matter where it comes from.

What can couples do to make their love life better? Before you start trying to repair your love life, you may need to repair your marriage. Is your love towards one another what it should be? The things you do to strengthen your marriage will automatically make your love life better. First, you must be willing to forgive one another. The Lord himself said, "If you are not willing to forgive one another, your heavenly Father will not forgive you," Matt. 6:15.

The second step is to look at one another in a new light. The person you married has forsaken all others for you. They have come into your life to share their life with you. They have faults and flaws, but so do you. Look beyond the flaws and dwell on the good things about him or her. A proverb of mine says, "Love cannot see the filth that covers a man, but hate sees the smallest speck on his garment."

In this spiritual dimension, you need to look at your mate as God does. He or she was made in the image of God. We are flesh and blood, but if we follow God, we are His children and created in His image. Therefore, you need to treat your spouse with respect as a human being that is created in God's image and in His likeness.

In a loving relationship, each needs to support the other. Each needs to play a role that compliments the other. Men and women are very different. They look at things differently; they solve problems differently. One partner has weaknesses in one area while the other has strengths in the same area. Generally, men are problem solvers. They get to the heart of a problem, to the bottom line. Women are nurturers and they lend support emotionally. Neither is greater or lesser because they need one another. It is like your hand saying to your foot, "I am greater than you." Each has a purpose and each is needed. An eye can see, the ear can hear and both are important. They belong to one body and each serves the other and helps the person accomplish great things. The two of you are one and you need one another the same as a body needs all of its members to function properly. In the eyes of God, there is neither, rich or poor, black or white, free or bond, male or female for all are joint heirs with Christ. While we are here, however, we do have to do things that we are expected to do. In the next life, there will not be male or female and no marriage. Matt 22:30, "For in the resurrection they neither marry, nor are given in marriage, but are as the angels of God in heaven." We shall be like the angels and not like mortal men. Our marriage will be to Christ.

Since we are judged by how we treat one another, we need to stop and think how we treat the most important one on earth, our spouse. In Matthew 25:40 He says, "Insomuch as you have done it to one of these, the least of my brethren, you have done it unto me."

When we realize this, and commence to do it, we will begin to love in the fifth dimension and if we love in a spiritual dimension, we will be joined sexually in that dimension.

Chapter 6

Tackling the Problems

As I said earlier, there are a number of things that affect a couple's life, which in turn will cause intimacy problems.

The first I will address is *fear.* Many might say, "Fear, I have no fears." Hopefully that's true, but in many relationships, there often times are fears. If one or the other has been in a relationship before where they were hurt, either physically or emotionally then they may have a fear that the one they now love will hurt them also. A person can be hurt emotionally and not physically, but if they are hurt physically, they also will be hurt emotionally.

If you have been married before and your spouse was unfaithful, this could be an issue. Even if you don't believe your new spouse might be unfaithful, there might be the fear that they will stop loving you. Being rejected for any reason is not easy to cope with and being rejected sexually or because the person doesn't love you is much more difficult.

I know what it's like to love someone then find out they don't love you. It is devastating. I always likened it to being a child up high on a ladder or roof and your mother or father tells you to jump and they will catch you. Then when you jump, they step out of the way and let you fall to the hard earth. After such a fall and the pain that comes with it, it will be difficult for you to ever trust them or anyone else again. Having your heart broken and crushed by someone you have loved and trusted is hard to get over. That is why many have difficulty believing that the person they are with *really* loves them. Even if they don't think it, it could be in their subconscious.

If this is a problem, you will have to face it. You will have to let go of that fear and trust your mate. They are not the one that hurt you before. They loved you enough to marry you and are with you now. If you have a terrible fear that they are going to stop loving you, you very well could cause it to happen! Remember what Job said in Job 3:25, "What I feared has come upon me, what I dreaded has happened to me."

I once made an analogy of people as being like monkeys with their hand caught in a coconut. Long ago, the way that monkeys were caught for the pet trade or for research was by using coconuts. The coconuts shells would be cleaned out and a small hole drilled in one side. Peanuts would be placed inside and the coconuts would be anchored to the ground by a chain. Monkeys would then reach in and get a handful of the peanuts, but then they could not get their hands out of the small hole with their doubled fist full of the nuts. Even when men ran up and threw nets over the monkeys they would not let go of the fist-full of peanuts so they could escape.

Many times, a person will not let go of their past in order to be free to enjoy their future. You must let the things go that are holding you back and keeping you chained down. You might get hurt again, but if you don't let go you are sure to be hurt. You will be hurt by loneliness, doubt, and will never be able to find true love. Even if you are lucky to find a good man/woman who will love you, you may be too afraid to trust again. If you do trust and marry, you could allow these fears that are haunting you to cause you to lose the love that you have finally found.

Sometimes fear can be a little more subtle than this, but the consequences can still be bad. Maybe you have low self-esteem because you don't look as good as you once did. Who does? If you are a woman and feel ugly, unattractive, or even ashamed of how you look, this can and will have a very negative impact on your sex life. Most of the time, it isn't even true. Often women look at other women and judge themselves by how a stick-thin model looks. The woman may then think, "That is the way I should look."

I am a man and I have noticed women since I was about twelve-years-old. Men want to see a woman with curves. They are attracted to shapes. This is a biological fact. In spite of what *you* think, your husband may think that you are very attractive. Moreover, if he loves you, you will be attractive to him.

There are many young girls and even adult women that are so caught up in looking thin, that they actually starve themselves to death. They cannot see that they are so thin that they look sick and are. It seems many do not know what looks healthy or even what is healthy. Men like women that look like a woman not like a pencil.

Even if you are a few pounds too heavy, or have a few wrinkles, if he loves you, he will look past the flaws and see the things about you that *are* beautiful. On the other hand, if he really loves you, and sees that you are letting yourself go and are not healthy, he will be concerned. He wants you to be healthy so you will be with him longer. He also wants you healthy and attractive so you will feel better about yourself. If you feel better about yourself then it will be much more pleasant for him to be around you. If you are happier then you will without a doubt want to be intimate with him more often, which will also make him happy. The same goes if it is he that has let himself go. You cannot turn back the clock on many things, but you can do something about your weight and some of the health issues that are caused by not taking care of yourself.

I have heard of women that are so ashamed of themselves and how they look that they will not let their husbands see them naked. Therefore, when they do make love it is in the dark. A man is visually stimulated, so this is not fair to him.

The next problem I will talk about is ***jealously***. A little bit of jealously can even be good, but a lot of jealousy can destroy the very thing you are jealous of. God invented jealousy. God is a jealous God and He says so many times in the Bible. He is jealous if His people worship other gods. He is jealous over Jerusalem. Therefore, jealousy is a natural thing. In the animal kingdom, many males must guard their mate or mates against other males. It is actually called "mate guarding" as I mentioned earlier. Men are also "mate guarders." There is a scripture that speaks of this. In Proverbs 6: 34 it says, "Jealousy is the rage of a man." This is speaking about the jealousy and rage a husband feels when his wife comments adultery with another man. It says that no amount of money or gift can take the anger away and that he will not spare in the day of vengeance.

Men have been given this jealousy to protect their mate and insure that no other has sexual intercourse with her. This instinct is similar to a woman's instinct to protect her young. In all of nature, you see the mother protecting her young even if it cost them their lives.

Jealousy is therefore natural, but it can be detrimental to a relationship if it is not tempered with reason and trust. You see this in the natural world among animals. Most often, a female that is paired with a male will fight off the advances of a rival male.

I have known women that are so jealous of their husband that they are constantly accusing them of being unfaithful. Many times, they are jealous because they are very insecure. They believe their husband does not really love or want them and would like to have someone else. This insecurity can destroy an otherwise good relationship. Often times, too, the jealous person will be so insecure that they have to "prove" to themselves that other men (or women if they are a man) would want them. In this case, the one that was so jealous actually becomes the one that is unfaithful. I have seen it happen several times.

My wife, that passed away, was not insecure in our relationship and she even had a bad marriage before she married me, where her husband was unfaithful. She had complete trust in me and knew in her heart that I would always be faithful to her. Because of this, she would often point out beautiful women if we were out.

Most women do not understand the way men think or feel. If a man was not attracted to a woman, then he would not have been attracted to them. As I said in an earlier chapter, some men just see women as a sex toy they can enjoy, and that is as far as their emotions go. A good man will still have the same desire as any other, but he will channel that desire towards his wife.

When I was a young man, I had as many hormones as any other man and sex was on my mind very often. I was married young and I was also a Christian. Every time I saw a pretty woman, I looked and admired all the features she had that made her look good. I did not want to displease God by "lusting" so I made up my mind to look upon any woman I saw as my "sister". This wasn't easy because I never had a sister, only two brothers. After a couple weeks of training my mind not to view another woman as being beautiful and sexy, it began to work. I could look at a sexy woman walking down the street in tight jeans or very short shorts and not feel attracted in a sexual way. "This is good," I thought. Then, however, to my surprise, my wife did not look sexy either. "This is not good at all," I thought. I then came to realized that God does not expect us to be blind. He knows, as well as we do, that women are beautiful. He designed them to look good to men. He mentions in Job that Job's daughters were the most beautiful women in the land. The *Song of Solomon* talks about the woman's breasts being "like towers" and she can attract any man." This means a woman's body is going to get a man's attention and he will want her sexually.

I soon came to realize that looking at a beautiful or sexy woman was not the problem; it was how I viewed it. There is nothing wrong with admiring beauty or even thinking the woman is sexy. The problem would be, if you wished you had her instead of your wife or take her from her husband.

You must know in your heart that even if you had the chance to be with this woman and never be caught, you would not have sex with her. You wouldn't because you have your own wife and could never be unfaithful to her. Even if you weren't married and she was, you would not have sex with her because it would hurt her husband. Loving your neighbor as yourself would stop you from doing to him what you would not want done to you.

I have always thought of it this way: If I happen to go to my neighbor's house and see that he is having fried chicken for supper, I don't want to take his chicken away from him and eat it. I would not do it even though I see that it is golden brown, crispy, very tender and juicy. I wouldn't do so it if it smelled heavenly or even though I knew it would taste delicious. Instead, I would go home and have my own fried chicken.

A man is going to be attracted to a sexy woman because he was made to do so, otherwise he would never get married in the first place. He just doesn't need to wish he had his neighbor's wife. He would not want to take her from his neighbor even though she might look a lot better than the fried chicken, smell better or even taste better. His wife has the same thing that his neighbor's wife has and he can enjoy his own wife at home. The Bible says in Proverbs 5:19 that you should always be "satisfied with you own wife's breasts, and be ravished always with her love."

Lust means to wish you had something. It also means to desire, envy, covet, hunger, thirst, long for, ache or yearn. One of the Ten Commandments says not to covet your neighbor's wife or anything else he has. It's not wrong to want *something like* you neighbor has, just not his.

Apostle Paul said in 1 Corinthians that it is better to marry than to burn with desire. Everyone knows that a man can be turned on and aroused by a beautiful woman. It is a fact of life and God designed it that way or there would never be any children born. You are here because your father became sexually aroused and made love to your mother who conceived you.

Being aroused or "turned on" is natural, but you do not have to act on it with another. You also do not have to act on it in your mind.

I am a man and I feel what every other man feels. Men focus visually on the parts of a woman. The more vivid the images a man sees during sex, causes the greatest organism. These images can be actual or in his mind. If a man's mind is on something other than sex while he is engaged in sex, he will find it difficult or impossible to have an orgasm. This is how men can slow down his orgasm so his wife can reach hers during colitis. Often, he will think of sports, what he might do the next day or something else. Anything to get his mind off the sex act until his wife begins to reach her orgasm. When she begins to reach a climax, he can again focus and reach an orgasm with her. Hearing her become excited also causes a man's brain to release chemicals that cause him to become aroused. Certain words, phases, moans, groans or sighs can arouse him. God designed it this way so they both can enjoy one another and reach an orgasm together.

A man cannot become aroused without seeing something sexy, hearing something sexy or being touched. His mind, however, can cause him to become aroused just by thinking of something sexy. Either seeing something sexy in his mind, hearing something or thinking how it would feel being touched in a sexy way. His body can even act on its own sometimes. This can happen during sleep. It can also happen when he is a young man entering puberty. His body then is changing and beginning to produce male hormone.

Since a man is visual stimulated, it can be a very difficult thing to control. Many of the best men have fallen victim to their own desires. King David, Samson, Solomon and countless others.

Women also have fallen victim to their own desires. Women can and do become aroused by seeing a handsome and virile man. They can become very aroused by thinking how it would feel to be in the arms of a man and feeling him make love to her. Most of the time however, women usually feel more romantic than men do. They want to feel loved, safe, secure, and beautiful. This causes them to want to be close to a man. A woman wants to know if a man can provide for her and her children. She wants to feel secure in that manner. You see this in all of nature. A male bird will bring food to the female over and over to show her he can provide for their offspring. Male animals fight to the death so the female will choose them to mate with her so their offspring will be strong.

Yes, you can commit adultery in your heart if you wish you could have illicit sex with a man or woman that is married. If you are single and the other person is single, it is just lust and if you acted on the lust, it would be fornication, not adultery.

The next topic is *anger*. We all have anger, but it is how we manage it that matters.

Anger can quickly get out of hand in a relationship. Sometimes a little remark can lead to a heated debate. Often an unkind word can trigger a flood of anger or resentment that has lain buried. Most times after an argument, people are sorry for what they said, but you cannot call back angry words. One of my proverbs says, "An angry word spoken in haste is like an arrow shot from a bow."

This reminds me of a joke I wrote. A couple was lying in bed one night in the dark and while they were talking they ended up getting into a heated augment. The husband said something the wife didn't like and she shot back, "Do I look like I have stupid written on my face?" The man said, "I don't know, let me turn on the light!"

We are all human and things get on our nerves, bother us, even the everyday problems can sometimes become overwhelming. Often, we take out our hostility and anger on the closest one at hand, which is our mate. There are other times a person can be angry or frustrated about something and their spouse thinks that they are angry at them when in fact it isn't true. I think this has happened to every man. He is working on something around the house, like a job that should only take a few minutes. Two or three minutes into the job of fixing the problem, he discovers that he needs another tool. As he gets off the floor after disassembling the bottom of the space heater, he begins searching for the tool he needs. He spends half an hour searching for the screwdriver he needs and can't find it. He is now getting frustrated. He didn't want to fix the thing, but now he is committed. He has other things to do or he just wants to rest. He could finish the task if he could find the tool he needs, but everywhere he has searched he has not found it. Then out of frustration, he asks his wife if she has seen it. He knows she probably hasn't, but it is possible that she came across it somewhere. Maybe he laid it down somewhere and she put it away in a place he hasn't looked. Therefore, he asks her, "Honey, have you seen my screwdriver? It's that little one with the blue handle; I can't find it anywhere." She can tell that he is mad because of the tone of his voice. Instead of realizing that he is frustrated about not being able to find the tool so he can finish the job, she thinks he is angry with her. She then snaps back, "Why are you mad at me? I haven't had your screwdriver!" He explains that he is not mad at her at all, but is aggravated at not being able to find the tool. She, however, does not believe him.

Anger can also lead to false accusations. You can hurt someone and cause a lot of damage when you are angry. When you are filled with anger, you do not feel their pain and you can inflict irreparable damage that can destroy the love between you.

A stranger can say many bad things about you and it may not bother you at all, but someone you love can say the smallest thing and hurt you deeply.

When someone you love attacks you in anger, you automatically strike back to defend yourself. It hurts very much and you want it to stop, so you hurdle words of your own. They have faults too and you are quick to point them out. A wise man once said, "He that is without sin, let him cast the first stone." You must be very careful when you start throwing stones; one could fall on *you*.

The Bible says in Eph. 4:26, "Be angry and sin not." The Lord himself also said in Matt. 5:22, "If you are angry without a just cause, you are in danger of the judgment." This is how God views having anger at someone. However, I think the best one is in Proverbs 15:1, "A soft answer turns away wrath, but grievous words stir up anger."

We need to apply this in our relationships. I used to tell my late wife when we had an argument that we should be careful what we say. I told her that someday one of us will lose the other and then no amount of wishing or wanting will bring them back to say, "I'm sorry."

It happened just as I said. She was only 52-years old when she got up one morning singing and happy that she was finally going to get the cast off her leg. She'd had minor surgery on her foot six weeks prior. Before the hour was past, however, she was gone forever. Therefore, treat each other as if it might be the last day you have to spend with them, because it very well could be.

Sometimes in our day-to-day living, we let problems weigh us down. Other times we are the cause of our own problems. All of us want to be happy and content, but how achieve it is not always easy. I once saw a talk show that was very interesting. This woman was on the program telling everyone how she overcame some big issues in her marriage. She said that the more she tried to get her husband to do what she wanted, the more he balked and did the opposite. Finally, after nagging him all the time, she decided to try another approach. That night when he came home from work, she met him at the door. This time, however, he was not met with the wife that was contentious and augmentative, but one that stood there in the room completely naked. As you might have guessed, this got his attention. Instead of browbeating him, she showered him with kindness and affection. After this, he would do almost anything she asked!

Proverbs 27:15 says that a contentious woman and a continuous down pour of rain are alike. However, it says in Proverbs 12:4 that a virtuous woman is a crown to her husband.

You might think that I am singling out women and putting all the blame for a relationship not working on them, but I am coming to the man. I have seen women that have a very good man treat him like dirt. I have also seen men that have a very loving wife, do the same. Oftentimes it seems that one or the other happens. There are men that have a very loving and caring wife and they mistreat her, lie to her, verbally abuse her and are even unfaithful.

True love is hard to find and the one that finds it is blessed. In Proverbs 31:10 it says, "Who can find a virtuous woman, for her price is far above rubies." This means you should treat your wife or husband with the love and respect they deserve. This life is short and true love is not easy to find, so it is worth the effort to nurture and protect it.

Chapter 7

The Unfaithful Mate

The most devastating event in a marriage is infidelity. This is a nice word for a terrible betrayal. It seems nowadays that a lot of terrible things are given nice names so they won't sound so bad. Infidelity, being unfaithful, being untrue, cheating, breaking the marriage vows or committing adultery are all the same.

Why is this so bad? So many today do it. It is difficult to handle infidelity even if you are only engaged. This man or woman has promised to marry you, and you believed that they were saving their sexual love for you and only you. If you are married, and have made a lifetime commitment to each other, it is far more horrible. If you have children, it compounds the pain. The most terrible pain comes, however, if you have given all your heart to that person, never even considered being unfaithful and have an unconditional love for them.

If you have been true to the person and have set your heart to love them until the day you die, if you would lay down your life for them, you may understand the severity of the hurt you would feel. In addition, if they are the only person that you have ever known sexually, it can be so painful that words cannot describe.

If you are this kind of man and find that your wife has had sex with another man, the pain is almost unbearable. You will see vivid images of the two of them together in different sexual positions. Moreover, with every flash of a different vision of them enjoying one another, the pain will hit you like a sharp punch in the pit of your stomach. The pain and sorrow will be so great that you will hold your stomach and bend over in pain. The tears will not stop; the grief is more horrible than if they had died. If they would have died, you could take comfort in the fact that they did not stop loving you and that they did not want to leave you. Having a spouse that is unfaithful, however, is like them stabbing you in the heart and then twisting the knife around.

I will not say any more, I believe you get the idea. If this ever happens, the marriage, even if it survives, will never be the same. If it does survive, the only way it will work is if the person that committed adultery makes the other feel that they are truly sorry. I've heard that it will take two to four years and hours of talking just to get the marriage back to where it feels even somewhat normal.

At this point, I think I should say something about how to overcome the hurt and grief of an unfaithful spouse. Many years ago, there was a distant relative of mine that had been married for over twenty years and his wife committed adultery on him. I grew up with this man and he was very soft spoken, didn't drink and was rather shy and reserved. He loved fishing and the outdoors. In my book, he was a very good man. After his wife left him and moved in with her new boyfriend, he could not handle the pain any longer and committed suicide. I didn't know he was even going through all this, because I then lived in a distant county and hadn't talked to him for a long time. If I would have known, maybe I could have said something that could have helped him. That is why I am saying this now.

The pain of an unfaithful mate can be so heavy on a person's heart that they may wish not to life without the one they love. I know how it feels because I was there. I even made up excesses for what they have done. Maybe they did not understand how much I loved them. Maybe they were going through something painful and didn't completely understand what they were doing. After I had grieved for months, I saw that I was going to literally die of grief if I did not let go. I had already lost forty pounds and barely got a couple hours of sleep a night. I then set my mind and heart to stop loving that person as a spouse. I had been faithful. I had kept my vows. I was not the one that had committed adultery. I had done nothing to deserve the awful pain that had been done to me. I realized that this person was not worthy of me. They were not worth me hurting and grieving for. They did not deserve me or my love. I also knew there were other women there that would appreciate me and love the good things about me. It was then I let go. I had set my heart to love this person with all my heart from the moment I took my vows. I would have laid down my life for them. Now, however, they had stopped loving me and I knew I had to do the same. It worked. With my will power and my faith (which is very important), I started a new chapter in my life. Later, I did find someone that loved me with all their heart. They did appreciate the good in me. So, if you have had an unfaithful mate, take heart. There are others out there that are like you and would be faithful and would love to have you.

If you are the one that has been unfaithful, seek forgiveness from the one you hurt. Maybe they will forgive you. If they do, be the best husband or wife you can possible be to that person because you have one in a million.

I have read that studies have shown that men and women face adultery differently. Oftentimes the man feels guilty and knows what he has done is wrong. Many times, however, the woman will put the blame on the man saying it was his fault and it was he that caused her to do it. No matter if this is true or not, adultery is one of the worst things for the injured party to go through. It will make the man or woman question everything. "Aren't I pretty or handsome enough?" "What awful thing have I done to deserve this?" "Am I such a horrible person that my mate wants someone else?" Am I not "man enough" or "woman enough" to please them? It can destroy one's self-esteem, cause severe depression or worse. Almost any wrong done by a spouse can be undone and forgiven, but you cannot undo adultery. That special relationship that you and your spouse had, has now been violated. The injured spouse will always wonder in the back of their mind, "Am I the one they really want or is it the one they committed adultery with?" "Are they better at making love then I am?" The list goes on, but you get the picture.

I will give an example of a well-known figure of history and his weakness that caused terrible consequences. King David of ancient Israel was a great man. He had fought many battles, conquered and subdued many kingdoms around Jerusalem. He was a powerful king. He was also a young handsome man and he had hundreds of beautiful women as wives.

King David, however, was a mortal man and had weakness like anyone else. He was a king, a powerful king, and he had an arrogant attitude. It is possible that he also was addicted to sex. The Bible says to do everything in moderation and you can overdo even a good thing.

All of his shortcomings came out when an incident happened one evening as he was walking upon the roof of the king's house. As he walked, he happened to see a beautiful woman nearby that was washing herself. She was so beautiful that David was instantly attracted. She must have been exceptionally beautiful with large, round, full breasts, long silky hair, very curvy hips and a gorgeous face. He had not sinned just by looking upon her. She was very attractive and as a man, he was naturally excited to see such a lovely woman. Immediately after seeing her, he sent for someone to ask who she was. He was hoping to add her to his collection of wives so he could enjoy her sexually.

Most do not stop and think, but there is more to the story than first appears. The woman was Bathsheba and she knew that King David lived next door and often took evening walks on the roof of the palace. It was no accident that she was there undressed, washing herself at that time. She knew she was beautiful. She knew that King David loved women because he had so many wives. She was a married woman, so she knew what turned a man on. She was washing herself so I'm sure out of the corner of her eye she saw David walking up there and began washing her sumptuous breasts knowing it would get his attention.

How do we know that Bathsheba wanted David? It is because when she was sent for she did not turn him down. She had sex with him that night. David knew she was married and she could have easily said, "Not so, my king. I cannot sin against my husband and my God." This would have stopped King David in his tracks, but she didn't say that. He was the king and she wanted him maybe as much as he wanted her. He wanted her because of pure lust. He did not know her so it couldn't have been love on his part. They had just met. She could not have wanted him because of sexual lust but because of power. She wanted to be the king's wife and live where she would be like a queen.

David was blinded by sexual lust and it cost him dearly. He had Bathsheba's poor husband, Uriah, sent to the front lines so he'd be killed. This was after David had gotten Bathsheba pregnant and he wanted to cover it up by having Uriah sleep with her, but it hadn't worked.

Because of David's terrible sin (which was worthy of the death penalty) there were awful consequences to pay. The Bible says, "Be sure your sins will find you out." Several other scriptures say, "God chastises those that he loves."

For the adultery David committed he deserved to die and for the murder of Bathsheba's husband he deserved to die but God had mercy on him. He suffered much sorrow for what he did. The baby that was conceived out of wedlock died a week after it was born. David's son Ammon raped his half-sister. Later, David's son Absalom had Ammon killed for raping his sister. Absalom also tried killing his father

David for the throne. Then to David's great grief Absalom was killed in battle. Several of David's wives were also raped by enemy soldiers in broad daylight. God told David that he had sex with Bathsheba secretly but his wives would be raped publicly.

David paid dearly for what he had done and he paid in full. God chastised him so that when he is resurrected he will once again sit on the throne and help govern in God's Kingdom during the millennium, Ezekiel 37:24-25 and Jerimiah 30:9.

It is difficult to believe that King David could have done something so awful. He was "a man after God's own heart." He wrote many of the Psalms, so if it can happen to him it could happen to anyone.

It is difficult to believe that King David could have done something so awful. He was "a man after God's own heart." He wrote many of the Psalms, so if it can happen to him it could happen to anyone.

I brought adultery up because sex is more than just an act; it is or should be a result of true love, unconditional love, not just an act that one participates in for pleasure. It is a gift to bring joy, happiness, pleasure, contentment and closeness like no other, but it is designed to be shared with only one and that is with your spouse in a marital relationship.

Chapter 8

The Joy of Sex

We now come to the end of the book. I have tried to explain many things about why sex is important and why it blesses a marriage. We are given many gifts and blessings in this life: sight, hearing, smelling, touching and tasting. All these senses are used in our lives every day and many times, we take them for granted. When we become an adult and find love and choose to make the one we find our partner for life, that is a great blessing. The greatest blessing, however, is being one with the person you love. You can love others; family, friends and children, but only your spouse can truly be one with you. Only your partner can give you children. Most do not grasp this. You, with the help of your mate, can create another human being, a being created in the image of God. You can also see yourself in this child. They are a gift and a blessing, but it is sex that has given them to you and it is God who has given you the gift of sex. God is the one that has given you the joy of sex.

When you are in the arms of the one you love and you feel that love and tenderness in their touch and see it in their eyes you will know true joy.

Many years ago, when I was working on my first book called *In Search of a Golden Sparrow* I asked a gentleman-friend if he would like to read it. The manuscript was not finished, I had not proof read it, it had many typing errors, but I wanted to know if he liked it or not. I did not know what was going in his life. He was a successful businessman, but I had no idea that he had problems in his marriage. A few weeks later, I met him and as he gave me the manuscript back, I asked him how he liked it. He then said, "It put my marriage back on track."

I knew it was an inspirational story, but I didn't know that it would actually change a life. When I wrote it, I actually prayed that it would touch people's hearts. It has and I hope this book does too. Yes, I sincerely hope that this book will help you enjoy not only sex but appreciate all you have been given. In today's world, many things are turned upside down and following our Creator is often laughed at. There will be a day, however, that they will not be laughing. God says, "God is not mocked, for whatsoever a man sows, that shall he also reap." The world is already reaping what they have been sowing but they, like King David, are blind to what they are doing. Some may wake up and realize that the Creator of the universe knows more than they do, but sadly most never will. I hope that some of what I have said has helped you. If not, I still hope you have enjoyed reading it.

When God created man and woman he said, "It is good." This is the fifth and final dimension of sex. I also hope some of the things you have read in this little book will draw you closer to the one you love. If your love has grown cold over time, it can be warmed back up. Step out on faith, have the courage to take that first step. It is worth the time and effort to bring love and joy back into your marriage if it has slipped away. Put the One that created love and marriage into that relationship. Put Him in your life and heart, for only He knows what true love is and He will share it with you. May He bless you with joy, contentment and closeness with your spouse and live in the spiritual dimension of love, which is to know the fifth dimension of sex.

About the Author

Kenneth Edward Barnes has been called, *"A modern day Mark Twain"* by a local newspaper reporter. *"He shows a Twain sense of humor in conversation and in his writing. He writes in the 'down to earth' style that Twain used to capture the heart of America."*

He was born on April 4, 1951, along the banks of Little Pigeon Creek in the southern tip of Indiana, downstream from where Abraham Lincoln grew up. As a child, he loved fishing from the muddy banks of the creek and roaming in the nearby woods. He never missed an opportunity to be in the outdoors where he could see all of God's creation.

Ken is a nationally published writer, poet and the author of over seventy-five books. Some of his most popular ones are: *A Cabin in the Woods; Mysteries of the Bible; Madam President; Life Along Little Pigeon Creek; A Children's*

Story Collection; Buddy and Rambo: The Orphaned Raccoons; The Golden Sparrow; My Favorite Poems; Betrayed; The Arkansas River Monster; The Coming Invasion; Barnestorming the Outdoors, and Do Pets go to Heaven? This could soon change, however, as he has recently written several others.

The author became a member of *Hoosier Outdoor Writers* in 1993, where he has won several awards from them in their annual writing contest. He has also been a guest speaker for the *Boy Scouts, Daughters of the American Revolution, Teachers Reading Counsel, Kiwanis Club*, and at several schools, libraries and churches.

Ken has been an outdoor columnist and contributing editor for several newspapers and magazines: *Ohio Valley Sportsman, Kentucky Woods and Waters, Southern Indiana Outdoors, Fur-Fish-Game, Wild Outdoor World, Mid-West Outdoors,* and a hard cover book titled *From the Field.* He has written for the *Boonville Standard, Perry County News, Newburgh Register and Chandler Post.* He has had poems published locally and nationally. One titled *The Stranger* went to missionaries around the world. The poem, *Princess,* was also published locally and nationally, and won honorable mention in a national contest. His best-loved poem is *Condemned,* and has been published by the tens of thousands. Nearly every single poem he has written is in his colored paperback book, *Poems from the Heart* and the e-book *My Favorite Poems.*

Ken has worked for an Evansville, Indiana, television station where he had outdoor news segments aired that he wrote, directed and edited. He also had film clips that were aired on the national television shows *Real TV* and *Animal Planet.* At this time, he has several short videos on YouTube and on GodTube.

Studying nature since childhood, he is a self-taught ornithologist and a conservationist. In 2009, he became founder and president of the *Golden Sparrow Nature*

Society, the name of which was chosen because of his first published book. Ken loves to share his knowledge and love of nature, and it has been said that he is a walking encyclopedia on birds and animals. Because of this, he recently published an e-book titled *Birds and Animals of Southern Indiana*. It has over 300 photos of birds and animals, most of which he photographed himself. He frequently updates it with new photos.

He has followed his dream of being a writer since 1978 and now lives in a cabin in the woods. Being an individualist, he cleared the land, dug a well by hand and built the house himself, which uses only solar electric. He even wrote a book titled *Solar Electric: How does that work?*

Comments on the author's work can be left on his Facebook page at: **Kenneth Edward Barnes**, or on **Twitter** at **Kenneth Edward Barne @BarneKenneth.** Questions and comments to the author can also be left at the **Author's Page** on **Goodreads**. All of Ken's books can be seen on his **Author Page** at Amazon and at Goodreads.

Books by Kenneth Edward Barnes in:
Paperback, Hardcover and E-book

1. In Search of a Golden Sparrow
2. Life on Pigeon Creek
3. Barnestorming the Outdoors
4. Invasion of the Dregs
5. A Children's Story Collection
6. Poems from the Heart
7. The B.O.O.K. (Bible Of Observational Knowledge)
   Under the pen name of ZTW

Books available as E-books only:

1. Birds and Animals of Southern Indiana
2. The Ancient Art of Falconry
3. Solar Electric: How does that work?
4. The Book of WISDOM
   (Words Instructing Spiritual Direction Of Man)
5. Instruction Manual for the WIFE
   (Wonderful Idea From Eden)
6. How to Care for your MAN

(Mate's Animalistic Needs)
7. How to Raise your CHILD
   (Cute Huggable Innocent Little Darling)
8. INSTINCTS
   (Interesting Nature Secret Tendencies If Nature Could Teach Secrets)
9. The Adventures of Ralph and Fred
10. Twelve Tantalizing Tongue Twisting Tales
11. The Eagle and the Hummingbird
12. The Grumbling Grasshopper
13. Buzz: The Cowfly
14. The Watermelon Turtle
15. I Don't want to be a Pig!
16. Who? What? When? Where? Why?
17. Buggies: (Also, includes: Animal Cracks and other jokes and riddles)

Available as Paperback and E-books:

1. Mysteries of the Bible
2. Christ: His Words, His Life
3. The Words and Life of Jesus
4. Why does God let bad things Happen?
5. Faith: Is faith in God dying?
6. A Rude Awakening
7. The Coming Invasion
8. Mystery of the Antichrist
9. The War on Christians
10. Death is his Name
11. Mystery of the Millennium
12. Beyond the Grave: Is there life after death?
13. Do Pets go to Heaven?
14. Evolution: The BIG Lie!
15. For the Love of God
16. A Biblical Mystery: Christians need to become a Jew: What does this mean?

17. Marriage, Infidelity, Divorce: What does the Bible say about it?
18. The Five dimensions of Sex
19. That's Bellabuggery: What in the world does that mean?
20. Thou Shall Not Kill: What does God think about the killing of animals?
21. What in the World is Wrong?
22. A House Divided: This is why Donald Trump won the election
23. I'd Rather be Right than Politically Correct
24. Gun Control: What's the Answer?
25. Abortion: Why all the controversy?
26. The Day that Time Stood Still
27. The Golden Sparrow
28. Madam President
29. Betrayed
30. To Keep a Secret
31. Ransom
32. The Black Widow
33. Flesh Wounds of the Mind
34. The Arkansas River Monster
35. Return of the Arkansas River Monster
36. The Capture of the Arkansas River Monster
37. The Last Arkansas River Monster
38. The Arkansas River Monster: The complete series
39. Outdoor Adventures
40. Life Along Little Pigeon Creek
41. The Long Pond Road
42. A Cabin in the Woods
43. Coincidences?
44. The Ruby Ring and the Impossible Dream
45. Kenneth Edward Barnes: An autobiography
46. The Book of HUMOR
47. My Favorite Poems
48. Buddy and Rambo: The Orphaned Raccoons
49. The Lost Land of Adreus

50. The Creature of O'Minee
51. Children's Stories II
52. Kenny's Children's Stories
53. Plays for Children

66096702R00062

Made in the USA
Middletown, DE
08 March 2018